. . . And It Tastes Just Like Chicken
Endless Retail Sales and Management Success

GREGORY L. WILL

Professional Publishing

Burr Ridge, Illinois
New York, New York

Sponsoring editor: Carol Rogala
Project editor: Beth Yates
Production manager: Laurie Kersch
Art manager: Kim Meriwether
Compositor: Precision Typographers
Typeface: 11/13 Palatino
Printer: Book Press, Inc.

Library of Congress Cataloging-in-Publication Data

Will, Gregory L.
—and it tastes just like chicken : endless retail sales and
management success / Gregory L. Will.
p.   cm.
Includes bibliographical references and index.
ISBN 0-7863-0194-5
1. Retail trade—Management. 2. Sales management. 3. Selling.
4. Management by exception. 5. Customer relations. 6. Success in
business. I. Title.
HF5429.W524   1994
658.8'7—dc20   93–5930

Printed in the United States of America
1 2 3 4 5 6 7 8 9 0 BP 0 9 8 7 6 5 4 3

To my wife Debra for her
unconditional love and support

Foreword

O ur society has created a passion for complexities. Everything must be new, different, or better! We feel things must be complicated to hold value.

Consider professions outside of retail. In the computer industry, new, different, or better ideas are being developed so fast that products currently available are already outdated. Who would have dreamed 30 years ago of today's accomplishments in the medical field? In education, teachers are constantly experimenting with new methods and theories to motivate students. And, where do we begin explaining the complex nature of our judicial system? On any given day, industries can be turned completely inside-out with new, different, or better developments.

This is not to say the retail industry hasn't changed. Every day we are exposed to new products and services, new marketing ideas, the latest fashions, and improved business systems. It would be safe to say that the retail industry has changed (new, different, or better) at the same rapid pace as other industries.

Our associates are often told, ''Your approach to retailing is too simple. Where is the latest secret to success from the top business schools?'' In reality, the cornerstone of retail's success has remained the same for centuries. Our success is based on two simple factors. The first is the relationship between the salesperson and the customer. Your abilities to become the customer's friend, qualify concerns, justify values, and close the sale are but a few of the components. The second factor is the relationship between management and sales associates. Management must be effective in determining and solving problems, delegating responsibility, and hiring, training, and developing personnel.

If you are not able to master these two simple factors of success, the latest tools from the top business schools will be of little use. In fact, if these two factors have not been mastered, attempting to employ new or better secrets to success will only create feelings of confusion and anger.

America was built on the theory and dream of "building a better mousetrap." We soundly believe in this principle. But the better mousetrap would have never been sold, nor the business effectively managed, if these two simple factors of success had not been the cornerstone.

You want and need things on which you can depend. Your customers aren't any different. If they can't depend on you, your products, or your services, they will find someone else to meet their needs. The latest secrets of success come and go, changing daily. But the foundation, two simple factors of success, will always be there—for you to depend on.

Preface

I n today's retail environment, sales and management associates must see the big picture of success. As they know all too well, the big picture is made up of perhaps hundreds of elements. Unfortunately, their hectic lifestyles don't allow them time to view the big picture often. But, fortunately, everyone is blessed with the ability to recognize their own special part of the big picture and, most important, their own strengths and weaknesses and how their contribution to success fits in.

> It is because of a person's strengths that they have obtained their current position, but it is because of their weaknesses that they haven't reached a higher level.

The retail associate must recognize and practice a management of exception philosophy—know one's strengths and weaknesses. Once the associates understand their strengths and weaknesses, they have a detailed directional map to a higher level.

Command of the current strengths must be maintained at all times. But concentrated efforts must focus on the weaknesses and turning them into strengths.

This book was written over the past 10 years by keeping

the management by exception philosophy foremost on my format. The selling processes and management obligations have been broken into specific detailed parts and sequences of events. To make this book work for you, you must complete a personal inventory evaluation of your strengths and weaknesses. After this is done, use this book to give yourself a pinpoint directional map to new abilities and greater success.

It is my recommendation that you read this book from cover to cover first, then complete your personal evaluation of strengths and weaknesses. Typically, a *strength* is something you are good at and enjoy doing, while a *weakness* is just the opposite. Rereview yourself and your progress every few weeks—make changes or add to your lists as the situation requires. Strive to make management by exception a part of your daily routine.

Is this principle of new success this easy? *Yes* it is! The hard part is developing the internal drive and determination to make it happen.

Gregory L. Will

Acknowledgments

S ometimes in the rush of business life, we fail to say thank you loud enough or often enough, but a special thank you goes out to the dozens of people who have influenced my life to make this book possible. Four business associates stand out as the largest contributors to my success. An individual thank you is extended to Wilfred "Bill" Janzen, Joel Friedson, Ronald Munzenrieder, and Jerry Johnson.

Not only were these four people responsible for most of my sales and management development, but collectively they passed on business philosophies that will never be forgotten. Their wisdom has shown me that hopes and dreams are larger than fact, to think big thoughts, that success is a journey, to never give up, to have courage, and to be a part of the solution, not the problem. Thank you, and my best wishes for your continued success and a long, healthy life.

G. L. W.

Contents

PART

I

Selling

Chapter One

A New Beginning

INTRODUCTION

A fter reviewing A New Beginning, you may find your-self thinking, It was too basic. I already use these concepts! But if you have ever experienced a "selling slump," you know the basics are your lifeline to success.

The sports world offers a parallel. When first undertaking a sports activity, it is imperative to practice and master the basic skills necessary to play the game. In scholastic, amateur, and professional sports, practice comes before the performance. This attention to the basics enables the athlete to perform in the arena—and, more important, to enjoy doing so.

The greatest challenge to those in the sales profession is that practice and playing fields are one and the same. The salesperson does not have the luxury of a practice retail environment in which to refine skills before entering the "real" operation. Like the serious athlete, you must dedicate yourself to the basics. The practice of basic skills must be an ongoing activity for you to enjoy ongoing success!

Whether A New Beginning serves as a refresher course or as an introduction to retail selling, make it your goal to practice and use the basics every day. Everyone in your organization can benefit from the material presented here. In fact, we recommend that it be required reading for all your associates.

Every concept, idea, or example in this book may not apply to your organization exactly as stated. Remain flexible as you adapt the material to your unique selling situations. Feel free to make notes in the margins, alter a paragraph, adjust a concept, or change the vocabulary—this is your book. Do whatever it takes to make it fit your personal style and circumstances.

UNDERSTANDING THE CUSTOMER

Instead of pushing, pulling, or dragging customers into a purchase, lead them! It is your responsibility as sales professionals to lead customers based on information they provide. It is amazing but true that if you give customers the chance, they will tell you everything you need to know to lead them into a sale. The more you listen, the better equipped you are to grasp customers' motivations to purchase. The data you acquire from listening is critical in leading the customer through a sale. Imagine this process as a dance: let the customer lead, and you won't get your toes stepped on quite so often. The first step in understanding the customer is to assess your listening and communication skills. Let's take an in-depth look at both listening and communication as we strive to improve your sales strategies.

Listening

The key to good listening is to focus complete attention on what the speaker is saying. Easy, right? You usually won't encounter any problems until you get hung up on one statement. At this point, you find yourself ignoring other statements of equal importance. You are so caught up in devising a response to that one single statement that important facts are missed. Or perhaps you become distracted by the radio, a crying baby, other people talking, or unrelated thoughts.

It is difficult to focus 100 percent of your attention 100 percent of the time. Some of us are naturally good listeners, others are not. Some are good listeners one day and not the next. At some point we have all been accused of not really listening and of only hearing what we want to hear. Let's face the facts: the more we have on our minds, the less effective we are as listeners.

Listening experts suggest three areas to concentrate on to improve listening skills:

1. Acknowledge that listening is difficult! Realistically assess your weaknesses in this area. Being aware of weaknesses will help you evolve into a good listener.

2. Situate yourself in a "listening ready" position. Lean slightly forward, get face-to-face, and come out from behind your desk or the sales counter. Avoid talking between racks or shelves. These simple actions prepare you to read the customer's body language, which will assist you in interpreting what is really being said.

3. Make eye contact! Good listening skills require both ears and eyes. Watch the customers' faces; note their eyes, lips, and expressions. You will be amazed at what customers tell you with their bodies.

Remember, you can't sell a product or service to customers until they give you information. The only way to receive this needed sales information is to listen!

COMMUNICATION

The first rule of communication is that if something can be misunderstood, it will be! If all the information needed to make a sale is provided by the customer, then your duty is to take this data and enable the customer to buy a product or service that meets their needs or wants. Sounds easy, right? Wrong! In the retail world, we employ words and terminology that may be unfamiliar to the customer.

Generally, every salesperson's first line of training is product knowledge. Be careful! You could dazzle the customer with your knowledge and then lose the sale. Why? Because much of what you say has no meaning to the customer, causing confusion and lost sales. This brings us to the second rule of communication: customers never admit ignorance. But they will indicate their inability to understand in another way—they won't make the purchase. When you describe a product, service, or business policy to customers, ask yourself, Do they understand what I said? If I say . . .

- 14-karat gold
- Solid state
- Single stitched
- Enamel
- Lead crystal
- 100K ram drive
- Oak veneer
- Polyester
- Ramie-cotton blend
- Air-cushioned insole
- Stainless steel
- Leather uppers

- Microscreened
- Vinyl

. . . do they understand?

Communication with a customer involves a series of four steps:

1. *Conception.* The response formulated in your mind is based on information provided by customers. You determine what you are going to say and how you are going to say it, so customers will understand.

2. *Transmission.* Thoughts can be communicated in a variety of ways, through verbal communications, printed materials, facial expressions, or body language.

3. *Encoding.* Now customers assimilate the information you have communicated. They listen with their ears and eyes and formulate an understanding, which may not be accurate.

4. *Return transmission.* The customers tell you if they understand what has been communicated. They may say yes or no, nod or shake their heads, or express through body language that they do or do not understand. Once again, trying to impress a customer with important-sounding words and whiz-bang product knowledge may backfire. Don't misunderstand—know your product! Some customers may want to know a little, while others may want to know a lot. Take your lead from the customer.

Remember, the rules of communication work both ways. Each party, the salesperson and the customer, is presenting and deciphering information. Continue to listen, and ask lots of questions.

Motives to Buy

Emotion?

Logic?

Or a Combination?

Emotion—Logic—Emotion

Do customers base their purchases on logic—the right color, style, or price? Or are their purchases based on emotion—needs and wants? While the logic/emotion ratio may be 50/50, 70/30, or 90/10, purchases are rarely based 100 percent on logic or emotion. Emotions play a larger role during certain occasions, such as holidays, birthdays, and anniversaries. Other buying decisions are based more strongly on logic. The principle is to avoid prejudging customers' reasons for buying.

Typically, the logic/emotion process has a set pattern: emotion first, logic second, and emotion third. Let's take a close look at this process.

Emotion first Customers will visualize the desired product or service. They may desire to look better, act better, feel better, or perform better—all of which may be accomplished through their purchases. Every product or service sold is a potential need or want. This determination of need or want must always come from the customer's perspective, not your viewpoint.

Needs are the basics, things required to maintain our lives as they are today. A key word to remember when working with needs is *replacement*. *Wants* are the extras, things we desire to achieve the lifestyles we prefer. A key word to remember when working with wants is *additional*.

This separation of needs from wants is important because the sales strategies applied in each case vastly differ. Knowing the right emotion—need or want—will give you the first bit of information needed to lead the customer.

At times, customers will divulge their emotional reasons for buying. They may say:

I need a new pair of dress shoes.

I want to buy a new VCR.

I need a new watch.

I want a new suit.

At other times, customers will not volunteer their emotional reason for buying. They may say:

I would like to see black dress shoes.

We would like to see your selection of VCRs.

Can you show me where your watches are?

I am looking for the size 42 regular suits.

Determining and fully understanding customers' needs and wants can be confusing. Customers may say *need* when they really *want*, and vice versa. Apply the key words *replacement* or *additional* and you may confuse the situation even further. Remember, take your lead from customers first. If they say *need*, lead them with needs; if they say *want*, lead them with wants. It's always possible to go back and change direction after further assessing the situation.

Trying to understand the customer's emotional reason

for buying can be a full-time job! It requires evaluating things as you proceed. Reconfirm, listen, communicate, and listen again and again.

Logic second After you have satisfied customers' basic desires of need or want by presenting products or services, they will move to logic. As customers move into the logic phase, things will change dramatically. Customers may have visualized the need or want, but now they must be able to justify making the purchase. Logic is justification. We are no different when we are the customer. When we consider making a purchase, we strive to make a logical decision. Unless we have more money than sense, we weigh value against price every time.

The building of value (logic) is accomplished through application of expert product knowledge and communication of features and benefits. Careful communication is essential in providing information that appeals to the customer's sense of logic. Once again, if you believe the customer will tell you everything you need to know, then you must also believe you can give the customer logic to justify the sale. For example, if a customer tells you leather uppers are important and if the shoes he is considering have leather uppers, communicate this. Tell the customer the shoes have leather uppers and then describe the benefits of that feature. As always, make sure the customer understands.

As a rule of thumb, the more expensive the products and services, the more logic must be added to justify the sale. Consider the purchase of a pair of black leather dress shoes. The shoes can range from as low as $29.95 to $750. What is the difference? There could be numerous variables, such as leather quality, designer, style, or manufacturer. If you cannot justify the price (logic), chances are you won't make the sale. Evaluating and responding to customer logic can be as confusing as customer emotion. Again, take your lead from customers, and then you can lead them.

Emotion third   The customer has moved through phases 1 (emotion) and 2 (logic). To close the sale, your job as a sales professional is to once again move the customer back to emotion. Remember, customers visualize themselves looking better, acting better, or feeling better—all because of their purchase of your product or service.

Understanding the customer is a full-time job. It is the main ingredient throughout the entire sales presentation. Some customers will be easy to sell—they will volunteer all the information you need. Others will make you work very hard for that information. Remain flexible and make the sale!

In summary, we have devoted our attention to understanding the customer—needs, wants, emotions, logic, and flexibility. Understanding these concepts will equip you to make more sales. As we discuss the five-step selling process in the following pages, we will develop a further understanding of customers' buying emotions and cycles.

YOUR FIRST IMPRESSION

The first impression you, the retail salesperson, extend to the customer can often mean the difference between closing or not closing a sale. A problem we face each day, even before facing the customer, is the stereotypes that have been placed on the retail salesperson. What is the customer's perception? Do you suffer from a negative stereotype, or do you prosper from a positive one? Retail operations and their associates are not the only ones stereotyped. Almost every occupation has a positive or negative stereotype imposed on it. The term *doctor* may lead people to assume this person is wealthy, educated, caring, or dedicated. A lawyer may be perceived as an advocate, a fighter, opinionated, or intellectual. A computer programmer may suffer from the stereotype of geek or enjoy the reputation of being a great problem solver. You may not be able to change a customer's first impression. But you should try to ensure that the customer's first impression of you is positive by considering the following:

1. *Smile*. To a customer, a smile is the most critical element! Many retail salespeople are champion smilers when the doors open at 10 A.M. But are they as congenial at 9 P.M. after 10 to 12 hours on their feet? Regardless of how tired you are, you need to smile. Smiling is contagious, and it communicates confidence.

2. *Enthusiasm*. Like a smile, enthusiasm is highly contagious! If you are not enthusiastic about selling your products and services, how can you expect your customers to be enthusiastic about buying them? Enthusiasm is momentum, so get some moving in your favor!

3. *Excitement*. This ingredient will create a positive atmosphere, which is conducive to action—the customer buying your products and services. Be excited that a customer is in your store with the intent to buy. Infuse your actions and words with excitement, and watch things start to sizzle!

Your first impression—a smile, some enthusiasm, a little excitement—will go a long way.

There is a way to remember the tools needed to create a positive first impression. Think of an *S* for Smile, an *E* for Enthusiasm, and an *X* for eXcitement. Give customers a little *S–E–X* when they walk through the door.

Is it possible to always make a perfect first impression? Common sense tells us no. It will be more of a challenge to put your best foot forward 10 minutes before closing. It will be more of a challenge when your time is consumed with other store duties. It will be more of a challenge when you are dealing with personal concerns. But remember, you need a customer to succeed. A few more customers, and you can be even more successful. A few less, and you may not have to worry about first impressions anymore.

Before moving into Parallel's five-step selling process, remember it is impossible to speak in absolutes. Be ready to make changes to fit your unique situation and style. Use this book to your best advantage—mark it up and make changes as needed.

FIVE–STEP SELLING

Selling Step 1: Customer Greetings

"HOW SHOULD I GREET THE NEXT CUSTOMER?"

A blank stare.
Please don't touch that.
May I help you?
Can I help you?
What can I show you?
What can we show you?
Need some help?
Yes?
Are you doing OK?
Let me know if you have any questions.
Ya?
Next.
Looking for anything in particular?
Help you?
I'm going on break now. She will help you.
Can (or may) I help you sweetie (or dear)?
What do you want?
Would you tell your little boy not to do that.

Does this sound familiar?

Salesperson: May I help you?
Customer: Oh, no, thank you. We're just looking today.

Salesperson: Make yourself at home (take your time, etc.) and let me know if you have any questions.

"No thanks. We're just looking." Do these words sound all too familiar? Unfortunate but true, these words are a major part of everyday retail life.

Customer greetings must incorporate the following three rules with every customer, at every time, and in every situation.

1. Acknowledge the customer within the first 20 seconds. An acknowledgment can be verbal, such as saying hello or offering direction or information. It can be a nod of the head, a simple smile, or a wave of the hand. The point is to let the customer know you are there and that you are aware of their presence.

2. Never prejudge the customer's spending ability. It is imperative to treat everyone the same! You may prefer to work with customers you "like" or who dress or behave in a manner of which you approve. Keep in mind, however, that all customers have money, credit cards, or checking accounts. Treat everyone the same.

    To illustrate a point, one company's president is quick to share a story from his previous experience. He was working the late shift as a manager at a jewelry store. Ten minutes before closing, two members of the local motorcycle club came in. Dressed in leather jackets and chains and sporting the usual tattoos, they seemed to be a young couple in love. His first impression was that he was going to be robbed (remember stereotypes?). But he went ahead and gave these customers his full attention. The couple indicated they had visited nearly all of the 17 jewelry stores in the mall, and he was the first to acknowledge them. Although they didn't spend much money (their purchase of a pair of gold wedding bands totaled $150), the floodgates opened. Because the young couple was so impressed, they told fellow motorcycle club members how nice the store was. It wasn't long before the store was frequented by other club members. They came in to buy gold chains, watches, anniversary gifts, diamonds, rubies, and much more. They became good, loyal, money-spending customers. All because they were not prejudged.

3. Never say May I help you? ever again! Instead, use related greeting phrases, such as:

How can I help you?

What can I help you with?

How can I be of service?

What can I (we) show you?

They all say the same thing—May I help you? Why shouldn't you use these words? Because they stop you in your tracks! You have nowhere to proceed when the customer answers your question with No thanks, we're just looking. The sales process has been halted. Salespeople have been conditioned to follow scripts; customers have also been conditioned to follow theirs.

Let's back up a few years from the late 1950s through the early 1980s. It used to be perfectly natural and acceptable to utter the now deadly May I help you? Business was booming, the economy was thriving, competition wasn't as great. All you had to do was open up for business, ask May I help you?, and ring up sales! In that era, shopping centers were not the focal point of a community. You could still count on customers coming into the stores specifically to buy something, not merely to kill time. Today we are told that over 60 percent of the people in a shopping center are there for no specific reason. They don't have an intention or inclination to buy—they are simply there. Because the shopping center has evolved into a social meeting place and focal point of the community (mall walking, lunch gathering, teenage socializing, etc.), methods in retailing must also evolve. If you remain the same while the customer base is changing, you will be forever trapped in the May I help you? zone, where sales are but a fleeting memory of the good old days.

However, keep in mind that today's lookers can be tomorrow's buyers. Acknowledge prospective customers, don't prejudge them, and try to avoid the words May I help you?

Another factor in effectively greeting customers is illustrated by the phrase "Friends buy from friends." In essence, customers will buy from someone they consider a friend. A business friendship between customer and salesperson creates loyalty. We want to buy a product or service from someone we perceive as a friend, not a jerk. Indeed, if friends buy from friends, then a customer greeting initiates the effort to become the customer's best friend. At this point, you are not selling products or services, you are selling yourself!

There are four recommended methods for greeting customers with the goal of developing such friendships. Different circumstances call for different methods; you must decide which works in any given situation. Human nature will direct you to the proper method. But don't sell yourself short: know and use the method that has proved most effective in similar situations.

In the game of golf, you choose from many clubs, basing your decision on the shot. This gives you the best chance to par the course. While you could play a round of golf with just a five iron, you wouldn't be able to play as well as you would with a full set of clubs. This theory applies to selling as well. Select the sales tool that best fits the situation.

Suggestions

Offer something

Compliment

Ask for an opinion

Conversation

1. Offer the customer something   This may include:

- Refreshments, such as beverages, snacks, or samples.
- A safe play area for children.
- Chairs for those accompanying the shopper.
- Direction to products or product areas.
- Information regarding promotions, new products, and so on.
- Package storage while the customer shops.

If this method suits the situation, consider the following offers:

Our clearance sale just started! Each rack is identified by red and yellow tags.

I can hold your packages while you look around.

Your children might like to play with these puzzles and books while you shop.

If your husband would like to relax while you shop, we have a chair and some magazines by the sales desk.

I can hold your baby while you try that on.

Our new spring (summer, fall, winter) line has just arrived.

This method of greeting works best for customers who look frustrated or tired, have children with them, bring a spouse, or seem lost.

Retailing giant Wal-Mart, which by most standards is a self-service retail operation, recognizes the importance of offering the customer something. Hence, the Wal-Mart greeter. Wal-Mart has taken one of the most congested areas of the store (the front door) and staffed it with a person whose only job is to say hi, smile, and assist with shopping carts or directions.

2. Compliment the customer The challenge in complimenting a customer is being sincere! If you aren't, you will come across as a handbook-memorizing, phony, insincere salesperson.

A valid compliment confirms something in the customer's lifestyle or taste. A compliment works best with repeat customers with whom a relationship has been established, someone with whom the salesperson feels comfortable. Rapport can be developed with a first-time customer as well, but it requires special attention to details to show sincerity. A customer compliment may sound like the following:

I like your shoes; they look comfortable. Where did you get them?

The watch you're wearing is wild! It looks like it will do anything. What are all the dials for?

Your dress is fantastic! You look like you're ready for a night on the town. Are you going somewhere special?

You should be seeing a pattern in the above examples. They all:

- Specifically state what you like.
- State why you like it.
- Ask a question.

Above all, remember to genuinely like what you are going to indicate liking.

3. Ask for the customer's opinion   There is nothing more unnerving than to greet a customer with a cheery Hi! How are you today? only to be ignored or treated with hostility. More often than not, when a customer ignores you, you think to yourself, Oh, they didn't hear me. So, you repeat yourself a little louder, only to be given a look that would melt steel. Sometimes customers will go out of their way to avoid salespeople or act defensively when they are approached. Remember the stereotypes that have been placed on you, and don't take things personally. It's not as if they don't like you—they probably don't like anybody.

When confronted by this type of customer, it is usually best to back off and leave this person to shop in a way he or she is most comfortable. It's a must! Inform other salespeople of that customer's preference to be left alone. Above all, confrontation is not the answer; it will only lead to more hostility and lost sales. The psychological profile of this type of customer is one of defense. The customer who acts like this is really trying to avoid salespeople out of a fear of buying and/or buying too much.

At a sales conference several years ago, the guest speaker was a champion insurance salesperson. He did not make his living sitting in his office waiting for potential clients to walk in. Instead, he became a super-seller by going door-to-door. He did not just go door-to-door, he specialized in knocking on doors with No Soliciting signs. He believed they were an easy sale. The super-seller would knock on the door and then begin relating to the person who answered (for example, by noting their grass was green and asking about their lawn care, or asking about the new car in their driveway). Once he had his foot in the door, he could lead the potential client in whatever direction he chose.

After these customers (the ones who hang No Soliciting signs around their necks) have shopped uninterrupted for a few moments without feeling threatened by a hovering salesperson, they are more willing to relax and feel comfortable in your store. At this point, you can approach them again and ask their opinion or ask a question. You may talk about old products, new products, a change in the store's layout—you decide. For example, you could start with:

Excuse me, but I was wondering what you thought about the changes we've made in our store.

Excuse me, but could you help me out? We have just received this new (*item*). What do you think?

Excuse me, but we just learned that (*manufacturer*) is now going to introduce (*new item*). What do you think about this?

Nine out of every 10 customers who ignore you or are hostile will tell you what they think. Asking a question or requesting an opinion is not selling. Without threatening the customers, it helps to relax them—making it easier for you to lead them in whatever direction you choose.

To this point we have looked at customers who have children or bored spouses, customers who are confused or lost, repeat customers, and customers who ignore you or are hostile. These customers will be 7 or 8 out of every 10 customers. What about the last two or three? We're glad you asked!

When you examine the first three types of greetings, they are really just ice-breakers designed to help the customer relax in your comfort zone—the store. The fourth customer greeting method will be discussed more thoroughly as it is the most difficult to master.

4. Conversation with the customer   The ability to create a conversation with a total stranger is much more difficult than it sounds. Try this exercise: Walk down the street and approach a total stranger with Hi, how are you today? Then, note the reaction. Does the stranger run for cover, answer your question, give you a strange look, or all of the above?

Starting a conversation with a customer is a challenge. Many salespeople feel that a good conversationalist does nothing but talk, talk, talk. Actually, it's quite the reverse. Becoming a good conversationalist is more a matter of listening and leading. Once again, your success depends on your listening skills. As you may imagine, creating a conversation is easier with repeat customers, friends, friends of friends, and family. But it is not impossible to start a conversation with a stranger—the new customer. Consider the following as you strive to become an expert at conversation with customers.

Before you start a conversation with a customer, remember the subject matter people like to talk about the most—themselves. Basically, we are an egotistical society. When we gather with family and friends, we are eager to talk about our jobs, our kids, our last home project, our vacation, and so on. The first sign of friendship or caring is to express an interest in others. Expressing this interest is a form of listening.

When you are with friends and family, this environment allows you to begin a conversation about any subject matter, including jobs, family, or the weird cousin you keep in the basement. When attempting to start a conversation with a customer, you should keep the subject matter on the lighter side. Think of your conversation with the customer as a low-cal lunch. If salespeople attempt to begin a conversation that is too heavy or personal in nature, they may be perceived as pushy or intrusive. It may look something like an old James Cagney movie: just imagine . . . the smoke-filled room . . . the bright lights . . . the hovering thugs . . .

Ya, see, so you're a customer, huh?

Well, ya, see, you're gonna talk, see.

We need to know, ya, see.

Rocko will make ya talk, see.

What 'bout those kids, see.

Rocko, make 'em talk.

As soon as customers walk in the door, make a quick assessment of them and their unique situation. Only then can you devise a topic of conversation to use in greeting the customer. How could you most effectively greet the following customers:

• A young man dressed in the latest western attire?

• Grandma and Grandpa with grandchildren?

• A person carrying packages from another store?

• Two women with name tags who appear to be attending a convention?

• A young couple wearing matching T shirts that proclaim It's better in the Bahamas?

• Two women wearing jackets with the logo from a local college sports team?

• Three young men wearing shirts indicating their loyalty to the latest rap group?

In these examples, there could be dozens of interesting topics to use in initiating a conversation. A quick appraisal of clothing and appearance provides many ideas. Look for name tags, baseball caps, T shirts, jackets, style, or fashion statements.

If we use the first example of the young man dressed in

the latest western attire, an opening greeting could be any of the following:

Are you in town for the rodeo?

Where did you get your hat? It's great!

I've heard about the rodeo; are you one of the participants?

Have you been to the Sage Brush? I hear it's the hottest spot in town!

In basic terms, any topic is good fuel for building a conversation as long as it pertains to the customer's situation. Even the weather will do. Only two topics are taboo when beginning a conversation: politics and religion. These topics are too controversial and typically spell trouble.

Another interesting conversation starter is packages that customers may be carrying from other stores. This becomes even more interesting if the packages come from a competitor! Accessories or other products/services you offer may be a perfect match for the goods already purchased. Ask to see what they have bought! Most people are proud of their purchases and will be happy to display their good fortune (a bargain) or good taste (a designer label).

Many salespeople hesitate to try this tactic. They feel uncomfortable taking such liberties with a stranger. A young woman attending one of our seminars expressed this reluctance. After being encouraged to try this tactic before passing judgment, she returned to her store and asked a package-toting customer what she had bought. The customer proudly displayed the contents and then promptly purchased another $150 worth of accessory items from her new friend, the curious salesperson.

Don't prejudge! Try a sales technique, a concept, a tactic first. You may be surprised to find it works.

Generally, most of us have no difficulty choosing a conversation topic. However, the real challenge is to continue to ask questions and to build the relationship into a friendship through the art of conversation. Building a conversation follows a pattern of questions, responses, new questions, new responses, questions, new responses, and so on. Examine the following examples.

A young man dressed in the latest western attire:

Salesperson: I have been hearing about the rodeo in town. Are you one of the participants?

Customer: Yes.

Salesperson: What is it like to strap yourself to the back of a 2,000-pound angry animal?

Customer: Well, sometimes it could be compared with riding a tornado.

Salesperson: How long have you been riding?

A person carrying a package from another store:

Salesperson: I see you have been taking advantage of the winter clearance at (*store name*).

Customer: Yes, it was great!

Salesperson: What did you buy?

Customer: These two sweaters, this skirt, and this jacket.

Salesperson: For office or casual wear?

Customer: All for work.

Salesperson: Where do you work?

Young couple wearing matching T shirts that proclaim It's better in the Bahamas:

Salesperson: How are you today?

Customer: Fine, but we're just looking.

Salesperson: You know, I'm just guessing, but I'd say you two just returned from the Bahamas! Were you in Freeport or Nassau?

Customer: Nassau.

Salesperson: How long were you there?

Customer: Two weeks.
Salesperson: Vacation or honeymoon?

(In the above example, note the customers followed the usual script—We're just looking. A conversation greeting can continue right through this potential roadblock in whatever direction you choose.)

A person holding a baby:

Salesperson: What a darling baby.
Customer: Thank you.
Salesperson: How old is he/she?
Customer: Six weeks.
Salesperson: How much did he/she weigh at birth?
Customer: Seven pounds and six ounces.
Salesperson: How much has your life changed?

Role-play with your colleagues, progressively making the customer/salesperson interactions more complex. Be nice to each other at first, and then throw in some curves! It's interesting to note how things develop and change as the role-playing conversations take different turns. This will help you prepare for anything!

The goal in a conversation greeting is to keep the customer talking long enough to learn about them and to become their friend (remember, friends buy from friends). Friendly conversation leads the customer into the sale. This process is known as "getting in sync." You are in sync when the customers start to spontaneously offer information about themselves in the form of answers to questions you haven't asked. You will know when you have gotten in sync. For instance, the following may occur:

Salesperson: What a darling baby!
Customer: Oh, thank you! She is the apple of our
                          eyes. She's about six weeks old now,
                          weighed seven pounds and six ounces at
                          birth, and will go to Harvard!

At first, the above example may sound far-fetched, but all salespeople have had customers like this. All you have to do is acknowledge them, and they take off like a rocket.

Salesperson: What a darling baby.
Customer: Thank you! I am looking at VCRs today. What can you show me?

In both examples, the customer offered information about herself and/or her desires without you having to ask. The customer is in sync. The more comfortable customers feel in talking with you, the easier it becomes for them to buy from you. Go ahead—ask questions and get to know them. Instead of seeming nosy, you will come across as genuine, sincere, at ease, and friendly. In fact, you will be perceived as the perfect person with whom to do business.

Prior to our discussion of conversation, we mentioned the experts' findings that you will use a conversation greeting with only 2 or 3 out of every 10 customers. But consider how important this is. For the sake of providing an example, we will assume 2 out of every 10 customers need to develop a friendship feeling before they will buy. We will also assume your close ratio is 50 percent, friendship sells one new customer, and your average sale is $50. Working with 20 customers per day, the following would be true:

Customers per day	20
New sales	2
At $50	$100
5-day workweek	$500
50-week year	$25,000
If each customer returns three more times during the year to spend $50	$75,000
If one friend of each customer comes to your store and follows the same process	$150,000

Let's take the above example one step further. How much did it cost in marketing and/or advertising to create these sales? Nothing! The sales were created from your abilities, knowledge, and skills as a salesperson. It's amazing, isn't it?

Of course, everything is not so cut-and-dried. Knowing how to greet customers with offers, compliments, opinions, and conversation is not a magic formula for instant sales. Years of conditioning will continue to take their toll. Customers are accustomed to hearing May I help you? and responding with No thanks, I'm just looking. They don't even realize when this transaction of meaningless words takes place. Even if you innovatively start the ball rolling with a more effective greeting, the customer will most likely mutter the tried-and-true No thanks, I'm just looking.

At this point, you must choose one of two possible roads: one, back away and give the customer time to look; or two, continue on just one more time and see what happens.

Many customers today are just looking. They are kicking the tires, waiting for the movie to start, getting exercise, or just plain there. Shopping has become a leisure activity. But above all, today's lookers are tomorrow's buyers.

You, the salesperson, must make the call. Having all the tools, skills, and knowledge to go past the customers' indication that they are just looking, you should first try pursuing the sale once more before backing away.

You will then need to move the customer toward talking about your products and services. In particular, this challenge will present itself when customers are engrossed in conversations. Once again, when customers appear to be in sync, you can lead them toward talking about your products and services. Potential interactions may include the following examples.

Young man dressed in the latest western attire in a women's clothing store:

Are you on a gift-buying mission today?

Tell me about the special lady in your life.

Young couple wearing matching T shirts that proclaim It's better in the Bahamas in a video equipment store:

Were you able to take any videos of your trip?

Did you have your wedding taped?

Your leading questions will direct customers back to their reason for entering your store. In most cases, you can assert complete control over the length of a customer greeting and/or conversation. Once the customer responds to product or service questions, move on to further pursuing a sale.

Often it will be easy to move the customer one step closer toward finalizing a sale. Customers will tell you what they want or need to look at before you ask. It's good to take your lead from the customer and begin presenting products or services, but remember, you can always go back to learn more. Take every opportunity to do so.

Habits are funny things; we are all creatures of them. It takes repetition of an act before a habit is formed or broken. If you review your own routines, you will probably find that you follow the same pattern of events or activities every day. Examine your last trip to the grocery store. Most likely, you followed the same path to make your grocery purchases, and you probably purchased the same items you did on your last trip. Habits are a method of operation, a way of doing things in a sequence of events or activities. Habits give our lives control and stability, which is why they are hard to break. To break a habit is to change something in our lives. We all know how we feel about change— we dislike it! With the best of intentions, you will probably return to your store armed with this exciting information, eagerly approach your first "guinea pig," open your mouth, and utter the unspeakable May I help you? Don't be discouraged! Change will not occur overnight. But with your resolve and lots of practice, you will make the changes you desire!

Selling Step 2: Qualifying the Customer

In the first selling step, you weren't selling anything but yourself. You aren't selling products or services in this step either. The goal in selling step 2 is to gather more information about the customer's desired product or service. Your key to success is to once again listen intently.

Read the customer's mind. All too often, customers name a "product" and they expect you, the salesperson, to know exactly what they want. Look at the diversification in today's products and services.

Tennis shoes: Running, walking, specific sport, leather, canvas, pumps, airpockets, high tops, and . . .

Men's suits: Single breast, double breast, wool, cotton, brass buttons, bone buttons, colors, and . . .

Watches: Quartz movement, auto-wind, numbered dial, day/date, moon phases, leather bands, metal bands, and . . .

We could examine any product or service and perhaps find hundreds of variables. We can talk with any customer and again find hundreds of variables.

Reading the customer's mind. Is it possible? Yes, if you ask the right questions. You can lead customers to their desire with pinpoint accuracy by simply finding the information you seek.

Selling step 2 will give you two critical pieces of information: first, the customer's emotional reason for making the purchase—needs or wants; second, the customer's dominant buying motive (DBM)—the end use or benefit of ownership. Examples:

Product	Emotion	DBM
Tennis shoe	Want	For workout comfort
Watch	Need	For punctuality
Wedding gift	Want	To be remembered
New dress	Need	For a big meeting
Engagement ring	Want	To show love
Desk	Need	To be organized
Book	Want	To relax

Remember, any product or service can be a want or a need, and it can serve any number of DBMs. These are based on the customer's perception. The following sample questions serve as a guideline for helping you develop specific questions that will be most effective in selling your products and/or services. Again, feel free to adapt the material to meet your needs.

Question 1: Let me ask you a few questions about (*product/service*) before I show you. Is that okay? This optional question obtains the customer's permission before asking questions about products or services. Ninety-nine out of 100 people will respond with a Yes when asked this question. Their response serves another purpose as well. It puts the customer in the yes mode at an early point in the sale—a definite advantage in the final close.

Question 2: Is this new (*product/service*) going to replace an existing one? Using the key word *replace*, this question will confirm the customer's emotional reason of need.

Question 3: Is this new (*product/service*) going to be used in addition to an existing one? The key word *addition* will confirm the customer's emotional reason of want.

As you become more adept at using questions 2 and 3, you will be able to combine them for a quick analysis and customer response. For example: Is this new (*product/service*) going to replace an existing one, or will it be used in addition to one you now have or use?

Remember, it is critical to confirm the customer's emotional reason for making the purchase—need or want. You will find yourself using different approaches, phrases, or sales tactics with needs and wants. Knowing the motivating emotion allows you to lead the customer in the right direction.

Question 4: What other (*product/service*) do you now have or use? This question allows you to determine what similar products/services the customer has, uses, or is replacing. Unless the customer specifically requests a duplicate product or service, try to avoid duplication.

Question 5: Is this (*product/service*) going to be used regularly or on special occasions? The objective of this question is to determine end use.

Question 6: How will this (*product/service*) be used? This question provides you with final confirmation of product/service end use.

Once you have gained experience in using questions 5 and 6, they can be combined for a smoother presentation. For example: Is this new (*product/service*) going to be used regularly, for special occasions . . . just how will it be used? Wait for the customer's response.

Questions like 5 and 6 will assist you in determining whether the customers' plans for your product or service suit the product or service they have in mind. If not, then you have that information now, not six months later when they bring it back for repair or exchange. Explain why the product or service would be inappropriate and suggest a more suitable selection.

Questions 5 and 6 are also important in uncovering the customer's DBM. The DBM is the actual reason the customer is buying your products or services—looking good, feeling good, acting better (remember the section on understanding the customer). The DBM will be used again when you return the customer to "emotion" to close the sale. You have now read the customer's mind!

Now that the general qualifying questions have been asked and the customer has responded, you can continue with other questions that may provide further information for closing the sale. You may ask about sizes, colors, styles, shapes, fashion, or other items related to your product or service. Let's examine the responses you might receive. What will you learn? (The numbers in the second column refer to the above question numbers.)

Product   **Response (What We Learn)**
Watch   1. Yes
            2. Replacement—the old one broke (need)
            4. Thin black leather band, yellow-gold color, black
               dial, no numbers, day/date feature, one diamond,
               quartz movement
            5. Special occasions
            6. Dress up, formal dinners, occasional work situations

You know that the emotional reason for purchase is need, and that the DBM is for fashion on special occasions.

Product   **Response (What We Learn)**
Bicycle   1. Yes
            3. Additional—BMX racing (want)
            4. Street bike
            5. Special occasion
            6. Off-road BMX race tracks

You know that the purchase is a want, that the DBM is having a product (bike) that will perform better in special circumstances.

Your proposed questions work well in the two above examples. But what if a young couple walked into your jewelry store to shop for a diamond engagement ring? Could you ask them, "Is this going to replace a diamond engagement ring you now have? What other diamond engagement rings do you now have? Will this diamond engagement ring be used for special occasions?" No! This example stresses the need for developing a series of qualifying questions that match your products or services.

Selling Step 3: Communicating Value

You now have the opportunity to sell your products and services. You've sold yourself and read the customers' minds.

Now you are ready to "talk product." Effective communication of value requires you to feel competent and confident in presenting your products. The primary purpose for communicating value is to satisfy the logic portion of the selling cycle. Therefore, what you communicate about the products/services you sell must be translated into something meaningful and important to the customer—value!

There is a danger in offering extensive product knowledge. It's risky to assume the customer perceives value in the same way you do. How you communicate is as critical as what you communicate. Remember our discussion on understanding the customer: If I say _____, do they understand?

In communicating value to the customer, you are working with "the big scale" approach. When customers need or want (emotion) to purchase something, they will justify the buying decision by weighing price versus value (logic). When customers first evaluate a product or service (the big scale), they generally view price on the high end and value on the low end.

To satisfy the customer's logic and close the sale, you must at least balance the scale. Price is equal to value in the customer's mind. Your goal should be to tip the scale even further in your favor by enabling the customer to see how the product's value far outweighs its price. To accomplish this, we will use features and benefits.

Features   A *feature* is a "truth" about the product or service. It is a fact and reality. Generally, it's something tangible that can be felt, touched, seen, smelled, or understood by some established standard. These may include:

- 100 percent cotton.
- Solid oak.
- 100 percent wool.
- 14-karat gold.

- Stainless steel.
- Genuine leather.

We typically find these features on care tags, drop tags, labels, boxes, or instruction manuals.

In addition, features can be added to products and services through store operations and policies. Rather than relying on the product alone, consider adding your store's special options to the customer's logic. These may include:

- Liberal return policy.
- Buying power.
- Layaway options.
- National locations.
- In-house credit.
- Special order.

Logic can be enhanced by reinforcing your store's special opportunities. Therefore, the product or service takes on additional value when combined with store features and benefits.

Benefits   The second aspect of communicating value is to declare a feature's benefits. Simply stated, a *benefit* is what the feature will do or provide. Adding a benefit adds value when the customer is seeking logic in making a purchase. The automobile industry provides a good example.

Almost all new cars have a window sticker. This sticker's main purpose is to provide the customer with information (features and price). You can read the automobile fact sheet and see that it has:

- Power steering.
- Power brakes.
- Electric windows.
- Tilt wheel.
- AM/FM stereo.

- Two-tone paint.
- Leather interior.
- Other options.

As a customer shopping for a new automobile, we may know we want the above features, but we may not know why. We may want power steering, but why? Because it makes the automobile easy to handle in every driving condition. We may want power brakes, but why? Because it's easier to stop the automobile. The salesperson adds value by describing benefits of a feature, justifying the price. The same system of features and benefits will apply to any product or service.

Feature	Benefit
100 percent cotton	Cool in hot summer months
14-karat gold	The best combination of gold and base metals, durability, strength, and beauty
Solid oak	Will last a lifetime; creates a family heirloom
National locations	Accessible service

When attaching a benefit to a feature, use the word *you* as a bridge.

What this means to *you*.

What this will do for *you*.

This bridge eases the transition from feature to benefit. For instance:

This item is 100 percent cotton. This will keep you cool in the hot summer months.

This ring is 14-karat gold. This gives you the best combination of gold and base metals for durability, strength, and beauty.

This table is solid oak. It will last you a lifetime, perhaps creating a family heirloom.

Our company has nationwide locations. If you move, you will still be able to receive service, should you need it.

It is important to separate features and benefits—describe them one at a time. Even if a single feature has many benefits, keep them separate and state them one at a time. This gives you the opportunity to add even more value. For instance:

Feature	Benefit
100 percent cotton	Cool to wear
	Easy care
	Quick ironing—looks like new

As a salesperson, you should be an encyclopedia of product knowledge. However, don't overwhelm the customer with all of your knowledge. Take your cue from the customers; if they say it is important, make it a key point. Be prepared to give either simple or extensive details.

Let's use a VCR dealer as an example. One customer may state that a four-head feature and remote control are important. Another customer may indicate that autorewind, four-head feature, solid-state innerworkings, clock, and autoprogramming and recording are important. Be ready for anything!

When customers decide not to buy "today," they will offer all types of reasons. These may include I want to look around some more or Oh, let me think about it. Nine times out of 10, this means the customers don't think the item is worth the money (value versus price). By refusing to buy, customers are telling you something about their perceived value of the product or service. Their logical justification has not been satisfied!

Another way to add value and balance the big scale in your favor is through the use of incentives. Using an incentive is like grouping features and benefits into a word picture that will tell the "big story." Basically, incentives are comparisons, nothing more than repeating the customers' desires by telling them what it would be like without the product or service. In essence, you must slip in the back door, not charge through the front door. For example:

Product	End table
Feature	Solid oak
Benefit	Long lasting
Incentive	"Isn't it nice to have quality furniture that will last a lifetime instead of spending more money replacing it every few years?"

In the above example, if the customer had said quality was the key in deciding to buy, the incentive would work. Once again, you have succeeded in repeating and confirming what the customer said. You are leading the customer through the sale.

Incentives will work with any customer desire. Read on.

Product	End table
Feature	Particleboard with vinyl covering
Benefit	Easy care, low cost
Incentive	"Isn't it nice to find an easy-to-care-for item that fits your needs without investing so much money?"

In this example, if the customer wanted an inexpensive item, you confirmed his desire. While incentives can be used for virtually every product and situation, try to avoid abusing them. Let the customer lead and use them only when needed or as a concluding summary in your sales presentation.

Selling Step 4: Desire to Buy

In selling step 4, you bring the customer back to emotion to complete the buying cycle of emotion–logic–emotion. By reinforcing the customers' desires to buy (DBM), you are using their emotions to create desire of ownership, thus motivating them to buy. In almost every situation, the customer must have a mental vision of ownership (use of, or benefit from, the product/service) before committing to take physical possession. To complete the motivation process, you need to provide a word picture showing future ownership use and/or benefit. Once again, you will accomplish this by leading customers with information they have provided.

Sometimes customers will provide or "paint" their own word pictures of ownership:

This (*product/service*) is going to be great, I can use it for . . .

This (*product/service*) is really going to solve my problem.

My husband/wife is going to love this (*product/service*).

However, it is usually the salesperson's job to paint the picture and set the stage. Sometimes you need to provide a detailed picture.

A young man purchasing a diamond engagement ring for his future bride:

> Just imagine. You're alone with your future bride at Divinci's . . . dinner for two . . . perfect wine . . . magnificent shrimp cocktail. You have just ordered your dinners. You're a little nervous, but you feel the time is right. You pull out this beautiful half-carat diamond solitaire from your pocket, and you tell her you love her so much, you want to spend the rest of your life with her.

A couple shopping for an electric blanket to give as a wedding gift:

> Picture this. It's 9 degrees below zero with a windchill factor of at least minus 65 degrees. Receiving this gift in the heat of summer won't diminish its value, because the newlyweds will silently thank you every time they snuggle underneath this blanket on a cold winter's night.

A group of men purchasing a custom-engraved beer mug for a friend who is being rewarded for having a perfect driving record:

> Picture your friend, and co-worker, after a tough day on the job. Now it's "Miller Time"! He pops a cold one and pours it into the special mug that you fellows gave him at the awards banquet. As he's sitting in his favorite easy chair,

relaxing, sipping the brew, he reads the inscription once again. Suddenly the day doesn't seem so bad after all!

A recent college graduate shopping for a new suit to wear during job interviews:

> Just imagine. You are sitting in front of the interviewer. You have all kinds of worries on your mind. Were my grades good enough? What does the expression on the interviewer's face mean? Did I answer all of the questions appropriately? Isn't it nice to know that by having the right attire, you have one less thing to worry about?

Other times, a few words tell the whole story.

A woman purchasing lingerie for a second honeymoon getaway:

> This will drive your husband crazy!

In these examples, the desire to buy was created by repeating the customers' emotional reasons for purchase through utilization of their dominant buying motive (DBM). While reading these examples, your senses—sight, smell, touch, and hearing—should have come alive. Your customers will experience the same effects when you use creative word pictures to promote a sale.

In the radio advertising industry, this technique is called "theatre of the mind." The television industry works with both sight and sound; the radio industry must rely solely on sound. As a retail salesperson, you can use all the senses to create a desire to buy (theatre of the mind). Explore potential opportunities to influence customers; in the retail industry, you have the best of all worlds.

In a real selling situation, word pictures such as the ones we've reviewed will not seem out of place or corny. In fact, sales associates just like you provide constant feedback that this selling step works! Many have indicated they thought the sale was lost until they created a desire to buy. Others have commented that the typical response from the customers is a glazed look in their eyes, a smile on their faces, and a nod of their heads.

Selling step 4 is tough for many salespeople to utilize because they feel uncomfortable doing so. If this technique is new to you, you will have a natural fear of something new. At first, try this technique using a few words or a sentence or two. Then, as you become more comfortable with its effect, add creative stories.

As you will have noticed, most word pictures begin with words such as *picture this* or *just imagine*. These opening words will help you set the stage as you complete the desire-to-buy step. You will find this an effective step in completing the buying cycle of emotion, logic, and emotion. Often, you will close the sale during this step. Don't prejudge. Try it—use it—have some fun!

Selling Step 5: Closing Sales

In the early 1970s, a group of college marketing students conducted a study that addressed closing sales. Ten students were each given $1,000 to spend anywhere they chose. Each student was told to try to spend the entire $1,000. They had one rule to follow: they couldn't spend any of the money if the salesperson did not ask for the sale. They were further instructed to return to their class the following Monday morning to fill out reports and to bring in all of the products or services purchased, as well as any remaining money.

On Monday morning, the 10 students returned with $9,722. Between them all, they were only able to spend $278. Although the students indicated they had found helpful salespeople, none of these salespeople asked for the sale. This study has been repeated many times at different universities and community colleges with similar results.

What happens if you follow steps 1 through 4 but neglect asking the customer to buy? You don't close the sale, and the customer doesn't buy your products and services. Closing the sale is the final step, a step which must be taken. You spend time building a solid foundation (becoming the customer's friend), asking questions, listening, and leading the customer to a desired product or service. You communicate value (logical justification) and create desire of ownership. It only stands to reason, after getting this far, that you should complete the process and ask for the sale. It sounds pretty easy, but is it?

Do you ask every customer to buy, regardless of circumstances? Closing a sale is the culmination of your efforts to help the customer reach a buying decision. After all is said and done, a sale is only lost when we fail to ask for it. In fact, at times you will be pleasantly surprised by a yes response when you least expect one. So, don't neglect the golden opportunity—ask every customer to buy!

The joy of no   One little word strikes fear in the heart of every person, regardless of their profession. This little word is *no*. Just the thought of hearing no will prevent many salespeople from ever asking for the sale. They would rather stand there and wait for the customer to say yes. Waiting is easier and safer, and they will never hear the word *no*.

The fear of no must be turned into the joy of no. We are, however, going against many years of conditioning. Early in our lives, we are conditioned to avoid no and seek yes. The word *no* is associated with negative, unacceptable, or bad, while *yes* has the connotation of good, praiseworthy, or acceptable. No is perceived as a reprimand; yes is perceived as a reward. How many times have you heard the word *no* in your life?

Many will say we don't hear the words "I'll take it" enough. Waiting for the customer to say this is driven by the fear of hearing the word *no*. Most salespeople feel their jobs would be much easier if every customer said, I'll take it! But being forced to ask the customer to buy makes you better salespeople. If the customer says No, I want to think about it, this is good (the joy of no)! Remember, you can't sell your products or services until the customer gives you information or direction. When customers say no, they are simply giving you more information and/or directions to continue the sales process.

If you believe the closing of a sale is nothing more than the process of helping the customer make a buying decision, then you're really closing the sale the minute the customer walks in the door.

Trial closes   Welcome to the world of trial closes! A *trial close* allows you to obtain minor victories or permits you to steer the sale in another direction. A trial close will provide important information to confirm you are on the right track.

Many of you are adept at making such statements as:

That color looks nice on you.

That fits you well.

This would make a fine gift.

Quality is important.

Your husband will love it.

The above examples are nothing more than statements. The

key to transforming them into a trial close is to pose them as a question geared toward producing a yes or no response. Once you receive a response, you can move forward or change direction. In either event, you receive the information necessary to succeed at sales. By adding words to the beginning, middle, or end of the statement, you can create a question.

Effective questioning words include:

Aren't they?	Couldn't it?
Haven't they?	Isn't that right?
Aren't you?	Doesn't it?
Hasn't he/she?	Didn't it?
Isn't it?	Don't you agree?
Don't we?	Wouldn't they?
Shouldn't it?	Won't you?

The statement "That color looks nice on you" is transformed into a trial close by adding "don't you agree" to the beginning or "doesn't it" to the end. The customer will respond with yes or no. In either event, you can now proceed, knowing the customer approves of the color, or you can change directions, avoiding snags during the final close.

In your attempt to deter potential problems from arising during the final close, you should use a trial close on every important detail. These details may include color, size, style, quality, or anything the customer indicates is important. When you get to the end of your sales presentation, there shouldn't be loose ends to tie up or snag the close. In the ideal environment, all that should be left for the customer to decide is whether to pay cash or to charge the purchase.

We know this will not be the case—the customer will hide important facts or decisions until the very end. Your selling experience will help you overcome many hidden factors. For example, through questioning the customer you uncover his desire to use a product for several years. Although the customer has not stated quality, it is a good bet that quality is important. If the product will last, tell him. Equally important, if the product won't last, move to a different product and tell him why. Reassure yourself that you are on track by taking advantage of every opportunity to use a trial close.

Another problem facing many salespeople today is the timing of the final close. Just when do you ask the customer to buy? It is possible to talk ourselves out of a possible sale! Knowing the five-step selling process doesn't mean we have to use each step every time. Don't overlook the customer's buying signals. Be prepared to stop talking at any time to close the sale when the customer is ready to buy. You will encounter two types of buying signals from the customer: *Oral* signals and *optical* signals.

Oral Buying Signals

1. Customers may ask for more information related to their ownership of the item.

   When could it be altered?

   Could you deliver or ship the item?

   Do you have a box?

   Can you gift wrap the item?

   May I write you a check?

   What credit cards do you accept?

2. Customers may express desire of ownership (painting their own word picture, based on their needs, wants, and DBM).

   This is going to be great! I won't have to worry about my suit and tie during my big meeting.

3. Customers may ask you to repeat some details.

   Could you tell me about the warranty again?

Could you discuss care instructions again?

Tell me about construction one more time.

For the most part, oral signals are very easy to recognize—the customer is talking and you are listening (information and direction). The other buying signals—optical signals—are more difficult to recognize. Up to this point, you have listened only with your ears. Once again, we are going to ask you to listen with your eyes as well!

Optical Buying Signals

1. The customer is wearing a big smile.

The customer is relaxed, at ease, and showing confidence in you.

2. The customer is nodding her head.

The customer agrees with what you are saying; nodding of the head also indicates confidence.

3. The customer is touching the product, reading or rereading the label, or looking the product over.

The customer is reexamining the product one last time.

4. The customer is searching for the right credit card, counting cash, or looking at his checkbook balance.

The customer is ready to buy.

Optical signals and other body language are important. You can read a person like a book, if you just listen with your eyes as well as your ears. You can tell if a customer is happy, sad, comfortable, uncomfortable, open, closed, confused, and so on.

For example, if a customer suddenly lowers his eyebrows and begins to stroke his chin, he may be confused. You could respond by asking, ''From the look on your face, you seem to have a question about what I just said. What are you thinking about?'' The customer can then respond without appearing uninformed or incapable of understanding. If the customer suddenly raises his eyebrows and leans slightly forward (an indication of disbelief), you can go into more detail to prove what you are saying. Several dozen pages of this book could be devoted to optical signals. Instead, we recommend that you read *How to Read a Person Like a Book* by Nierenberg and Caleno.

IN CONCLUSION

We hope this material has refreshed your memory, reconfirmed some ideas, and, perhaps, introduced new concepts to add to your sales techniques. It takes time to make adjustments to the course of success. Don't expect immediate results. Be patient, persevere, and continue to think in the long term. Change and improvement are some of the greatest challenges we face; they also provide some of the greatest rewards and satisfactions. We encourage you to continue your selling education whenever the opportunity arises. Attend seminars, read books, listen to audiotapes, and view videos. Even if the materials are not specific to the retail industry, the particulars can be adjusted. Remain flexible, and make the system work for you! Good luck and good selling!

Chapter Two

A Dominating Position

INTRODUCTION

T wo pictures come to mind when we hear the words *retail salesperson:* a clerk or a professional. When we take the opportunity to look at a retailer, it's hard to determine which one he or she really is. What separates a clerk from a professional? Is it the manner of dress, manner of speech, or perhaps the manner of actions?

The above factors, and many others, are important components of a first impression. However, a lasting impression is based on the attitude and confidence you possess and project! You may be able to talk the talk, but can you walk the walk? Your attitude and level of confidence shows in everything you do.

These two areas will either provide the opportunity for positive results or they will hinder your success. If your attitude is I can, and you achieve success in a certain situation, you create confidence. When you don't create confidence, you are less likely to be motivated to seek additional knowledge and skill. In essence, you avoid the situation.

We are trained to react to things in a specific manner,

and this training often develops into habits. These habitual reactions are based on outside information, as well as personal knowledge, experience, and past success. Are your habits projecting a professional, positive image? Or do you present yourself as a clerk?

Many salespeople have had the unfortunate experience of being accused of being a "born salesperson." This accusation is unlikely to be valid. Just moments after birth, not a single one of these born salespeople turned to the doctor or nurse and said, "Will that be cash or charge?"

The following pages cover three key concepts that have proven effective in increasing personal sales as well as overall business sales. Learn to master these concepts and you will not only reach the top, you will stay there! We are confident that putting these three concepts into practice will provide the opportunity to boost your sales by as much as 30 percent. Aspiring to obtain a 30 percent sales increase in any retail market is a very bold and dramatic step to take. For many salespeople, an increase of this size would be nothing shy of a miracle.

Achieving any sales increase is a two-school-of-thought process. First, you tell yourself, If I could increase daily traffic flow, sales would increase. After all, we live in a world ruled by the law of averages and numbers. If you are able to sell every 3 or 4 customers out of each 10, an easy solution to increasing sales would be to have more people walk through the front door. But this is very expensive. Most companies spend an average customer's first purchase just to get them into the front door.

If your average customer spends $50 and you need 10,000 new customers to reach the 30 percent sales increase goal, you would need to spend $500,000. And spending the additional money doesn't guarantee additional sales. It would be very difficult to convince the marketing department to spend the additional funds.

The second school of thought involves you, the salesperson, being more effective (professional) in working with current customers. After close examination of the existing situation, you should realize that the customers are already there spending money. All you have to do is convince them to buy a little bit more, overcome their objections, or close the sale—attitude and confidence.

Before you dive into the three key concepts, we ask you to keep two points in mind:

1. You must realize these concepts come into play only after you have taken the customer through a five-step selling process (greeting, qualifying, communicating value, creating desire of ownership, and closing the sale/setting the stage for closing).

2. As an example, we will use $25 as an average sale throughout the three sections. To make these numbers work for you, use $25 as 100 percent and make adjustments to your actual situation to reach the same goals and percentages (example: if your average sale is $12.50, cut the numbers in half; if your average sale is $50, double the numbers).

MULTIPLE/SUGGESTIVE SELLING

It's not a question of *if* customers will buy additional products, it's only a question of *what* they will buy! This is a bold assumption, but it is an attitude you must possess to be successful. Multiple, or suggestive, selling of accessories or add-on items is one of the fastest and most cost-effective ways to increase your personal sales and the store's sales. Customers have already committed to buying a product or service. Your objective is to keep them in their buying mode long enough to convince them to buy just a little bit more.

Keep in mind, you are not trying to double, triple, or quadruple their purchase. Generally, a small percentage of the main purchase is all that's necessary to do dramatic

Multiple Selling

Main purchase	
Gross sale	$25.00
Product cost	12.50
Gross profit	12.50
Costs/Expenses	
Salary and benefits	$2.90
Telephone	.64
Rent	1.64
Utilities	.37
Home office cost	1.17
Advertising	1.60
Bank charges	.28
Miscellaneous	1.40
Total cost/expense	$10.00
Net profit (loss)	$ 2.50
Accessory purchase	
Gross sale	$5.00
Product cost	2.50
Gross profit	2.50
Costs/Expenses	
None (absorbed by main purchase)	
Net profit (loss) of accessory	2.50
Total net profit (loss)	$5.00

things to your overall sales—and the store's bottom-line profit.

As you review the above example, you can see the net profit of the main purchase is significantly lower than the multiple/accessory purchase due to the store's operating costs and expenses. The multiple/accessory purchase generated a greater profit because the store's operating costs and expenses had already been absorbed by the main purchase. Therefore, the net profit rises, often doubles or triples, with a very small additional sale.

Your company's home offices, regional managers, district managers, and/or owners highly regard a sales associate's ability to multiple sell (sell accessories) with a main product or service. Often the store's or company's profits and/or ranking are determined by the extra accessory sales.

Several years ago, we were asked by a furniture retailer to examine its top five stores and determine where the differences were. Initial observation indicated the total amount of money separating the number one store from number five was only $2,738. A graph was created to target various departments—dining room, bedding, living room, bedroom furniture, end tables, lamps, and so on—and each store's department sales totals were compared. The five stores almost matched each other dollar for dollar in the main categories, with the difference in sales from number one to number five reduced to only $523. The remaining difference of $2,215 was in the "accessory" categories—lamps, pictures, and Scotchgarding.

As we further investigated each store and the special accessory categories, the difference between number one and number two was only $117.95. This difference equated to one pair of lamps at $49.95 and one Scotchgarding at $68. What really made these numbers amazing were the stores' total sales. Each of the top five stores recorded over $1.2 million in sales during the previous 12 months.

Many retailers have devoted manuals and thousands of hours of training toward assisting their sales associates to become better at multiple or suggestive selling. Some have developed abbreviations to help associates remember key sales terminology. They include:

MPH—multiples per hour	PTA—potential to ask
ESP—extra sales potential	SOS—save our store
SET—suggest every transaction	BVDs—better volume decisions

Regardless of the method (remembering abbreviations, understanding the system, or both), two concerns about asking customers to buy more are commonly expressed. They are timing and method of asking.

Timing

A fine line separates customers' purchasing and non-purchasing modes. If you wait until customers are at the sales counter ready to finalize their main purchase before asking for the additional sale, they may have decided not to spend any more money and are probably no longer in a purchasing mode.

Failure to ask for additional purchases at the appropriate time is one reason why so many stores have resorted to placing merchandise (accessories) at or near the sales counter, where they become impulse items. Items displayed at the counter area are there to create impulse buying. The goal is to motivate the customer to make an additional purchase without relying on sales associates' job performance. Even self-service businesses like Wal-Mart, Kmart, Target, and Giant have lined their checkout stands with merchandise. They want extra sales!

It is critical to approach customers with accessories to a main purchase item while they are still shopping. At the least, a salesperson should approach a customer with additional potential items as soon as an initial buying decision has been made. Suggested accessories could include:

Main Product	Accessories
Man's dress shirt	Tie, cuff links, tie bar
Woman's sweater	Earrings, necklace, bracelet, scarf, pin
Tennis shoes	Sweatsocks, shoe cleaner, extra laces, sports bag
Diamond earrings	Jewelry cleaner, travel bag, jewelry box
Sofa and chair	End tables, coffee tables, lamps, Scotch-garding, "sleeper," throw pillows
Videotape (movie)	Storage rack, VCR head cleaner, tape rewinder, remote control batteries

The best time to begin selling accessory items is the moment the customer walks in the door! Strive to complete the "picture" of ownership with not only the main purchase but with the accessory items as well. This is really an issue of attitude and confidence. You must believe it is not a question of whether the customer is going to buy, but only a question of what they are going to buy.

Method of Asking

The way you ask a customer to buy additional products and services (accessories) is a sensitive subject matter. Often, a salesperson won't even approach a customer with accessories because of fear of blowing the entire sale. This is typical of new salespeople. Once a new salesperson's habit of not asking for the sale is broken, the salesperson will move on to the next phase and will approach the subject in the following manner:

Would you like to look at . . . ?

Do you need . . . ?

Would you like some . . . to go with . . . ?

Can I show you some . . . ?

By posing a question unlikely to generate a yes response, they are giving the customer an opportunity to say no and a way out! Again, the salesperson feels she must give the customer a way out to protect the main purchase.

Once more, it is an issue of attitude and confidence. First you develop the confidence to make the sale, and so you are comfortable and happy. When you are asked to do something more or different, you often need an attitude adjustment (or prior success in a similar situation) before you will incorporate new ideas or actions into your sales approach. To change your attitude, increase your confidence levels, and be in a position to succeed at multiple suggestive selling, you must concentrate on (and strive for perfection in) the following three areas. **First**, be prepared (the matching game)! This oft-repeated statement is crucial! Review the store daily for new arrivals and learn all you can about the products and services as soon as they become available to the buying public. Play the matching game before the sales process begins. If you don't, you may be grasping for inappropriate products and services during selling time.

We all enjoyed this activity when we first started our jobs in the retail industry. It was fun and exciting to survey the merchandise and play the matching game. After a while, though, the sights may become too familiar and lack their initial appeal. You may fail to notice new products and services or their match-up potential. You may continue in a comfortable habit of ''selling'' on the customer's terms rather than directing and leading the sale from a position of strength.

This position of sameness is similar to our morning and evening drive to and from the store. At first, we noticed every detail—the stop signs, the lights, the construction projects, the restaurants, the gas stations. Later, after repeating this drive several times, we were able to ignore the details. In fact, our journey becomes so automatic that we may not even be aware of how we arrived at our final destination. The sights become so commonplace, they don't even elicit a reaction.

Sameness endangers your ability to successfully sell additional products and services. Therefore, logic would suggest you make a daily concentrated effort to increase your awareness of the store and its products, services, and accessory items. Even if you had the opportunity to close the store the night before, take the time to review the situation and play the matching game just one more time before you start your hectic, busy day.

Second, motivate the customer to buy! Having accessories to sell doesn't mean a customer will necessarily buy them. It's still your job to motivate the customer to see the value in making such a purchase.

All too often we become caught up in the "product and service" trap. Remember, customers will make their purchases based on emotion—after their logical justification has been satisfied. Customers won't buy what you are selling! Instead, they buy what the products and services will do for them. For instance:

Don't sell clothing—sell style, fashion, color, appearance, special occasions, and relaxation.

Don't sell toys—sell happy moments, smiles, learning, new confidence, or development.

Don't sell jewelry—sell love, happiness, investment, beauty, success, or style.

Don't sell athletic shoes—sell running, walking, exercise, stress relief, comfort, or health.

Don't sell food—sell fresh, hot or cold, tasty, nutritious, or healthy.

Don't sell things—sell ideas, emotions, feelings, life, problem solving, or concepts.

Although the above examples have highlighted a main product in their descriptions, this same theory must be used when selling accessory items. Remember, the customer will buy emotionally after logical reasoning has been satisfied.

If you have been successful at uncovering customers' needs and wants and are aware of the actual usage of the products and services, you can appeal to their purchasing mode by creating a picture of ownership. The picture is completed with the accessory items. The objective is to transform what you sell into what it will do for the customer.

Sometimes you can use the silent approach. Many salespeople include the accessories without saying a word. Include accessories as a part of the main product or service sale or be more creative. A female salesperson had the un-matched ability to sell packages of argyle socks to 9 out of every 10 customers. She even sold argyle socks to custom-ers who didn't buy shoes. The sales were made without her saying a word. Read on to learn her technique:

> Several years ago, *Cosmopolitan* magazine featured an article titled "How to Tell If Your Man Is One of the Last of the Red-Hot Lovers? Argyle Socks." She cut out the title page of the article and had it laminated. Whenever she had cus-tomers (men or women) trying on a pair of shoes, she would excuse herself from the sale, grab two packages of argyle socks, and hand them to the customers along with the lami-nated article. She then allowed the customers to make their own decision.

Generally, you must use the verbal approach. Remem-ber, the customer will buy what the products and services will do for them. If you have uncovered the customer's intended use or uses of the product or service, you have all the information you need to create a desire for the accesso-ries.

Creating a word picture, as many salespeople know, is one of the most effective tools of your sales presentation. Motivating customers to buy accessories takes nothing more than showing them how they can enhance the use of your products or services. The following examples were submitted by sales associates.

A stereo store salesperson working with a customer purchasing a portable stereo boom box:

> Just imagine. It's Saturday afternoon at the park. You are there with all of your friends having a cookout. The Frisbees are flying, the burgers are sizzling on the grill, the music is great. Suddenly the music begins to fade out. After in-specting your new stereo, you discover the batteries have lost their charge. Now, you jump into your car, drive to a store, purchase new batteries, get back into your car, drive

back to the park, and try to get back into the fun. Wouldn't it be better if you had the extra power source with you? Would you like the standard battery 4-pack, the economy 12-pack, or an adapter?

A plant store where an observant salesperson has great success selling additional pots, soil, and fertilizer with many of the main plant sales:

Just imagine. It's about six months from now. You've watched your new plant bloom and grow. It's really become a part of your home. However, the only way to assure you'll continue to enjoy its beauty and to help it grow is to repot it. If you're anything like me, you probably get the urge to pot plants around 10:30 P.M. when all the stores are closed. We want to tackle those projects whenever the mood strikes us. Wouldn't it be great if you had all the supplies you needed on hand, the fertilizer, soil, and pots, so you could do the job whenever it was convenient for you?

The salesperson would show a variety of pots, fertilizers, and soils. He would then proceed to ask you, the customer, what size pot or which type of fertilizer or potting soil you would like, making it easy for you to buy something. Since the accessory items in this case usually cost more than the plant itself, the profit margin is greatly increased.

A bakery store that sells coffee and baked goods as well as accessory items, such as coffee decanters and cookie canisters:

The salesperson asks the customer, "Do you ever take day-long driving trips?" After an affirmative response from the customer, the salesperson continues by asking the customer about the color of her car's interior. After eliciting a response, the salesperson invites the customer to take a coffee decanter that coordinates with her car interior right off the shelf behind her. The sales associate then explains how the decanter would keep a beverage hot or cold and keep it from spilling and ruining the interior of the customer's car. The salesperson also notes that the color of the decanter coordinates with the customer's car interior. Each decanter comes with a coupon for a free pot of coffee, increasing motivation to buy.

Cookie canisters are presented in a similar fashion. Canisters with special occasion or holiday motifs are placed strategically on shelves and counters. When a dozen cookies or more are purchased, the salesperson asks the customer to hand him a canister, then proceeds to explain how great the canisters are for gift giving or as a convenient place to store cookies at home. Inside each canister is a coupon for a dozen free cookies. In both instances, the cost of the decanter or the canister is 10 to 20 times the value of the main purchase. Sales are easily increased with little additional cost to the bakery.

A clothing store where most customers who come in to try on new outfits are not wearing the proper accessories. They don't have the right shoes, tie, shirt, jacket, or other accessories to complete the look:

Smart sales associates never let the customer into the dressing room with only one item of clothing. First, they find out how, when, where, and why the item is going to be worn or used. They also inquire about accessories the customer may already own that will coordinate with the clothing. Escorting the customer to the dressing room, the salesperson says, "I'll be right back." After quickly finding the perfect accessories, the salesperson takes them to the dressing room. The customer is then able to try on the entire ensemble before looking in the mirror.

A $70 skirt sale can be increased to $125 or more with the addition of choice accessories presented at the appropriate time. Many men's stores have extra white shirts and brown or black shoes in various sizes to help a customer envision the whole look when trying on the clothing. By dressing in a suit complete with shirt, tie, pocket square, cuff links, belt, and shoes, the customer can appreciate the entire effect and will usually purchase some of the additional accessories.

A shoe store where it is standard policy for salespeople to find out the customer's planned use for the product and then relate it back to him as a tool in their multiple selling:

> Picture this. It's six months from now, and you have another big meeting. Your suit and shirt are still perfect, you're wearing the ivory tie, and you've just had a great haircut. You're happy with your appearance and the image you will present at the meeting. Then you notice that your shoes are scuffed, dirty, and in need of polishing. Wouldn't it be nice to have the right polish at home so you could put on the perfect shine at 11 PM while you're making those last-minute preparations before the meeting in the morning?

Another example:

> It's 6:30 AM and, as you're dressing in your best suit, preparing for a big business meeting, you discover a run in your nylons. This always seems to happen at the worst possible time. Although you selected the perfect nylons for your suit and shoes, wouldn't it be wise to have an extra pair or two on hand for those unexpected times when you can least afford such an inconvenience?

The customer's eyes will do all the talking for you. Specifically, you don't always have to tell the customer about all of the accessories. Allow the customer to see the accessories first. If there is no response, you can then provide a detailed explanation about the benefits of owning the accessories.

Third, make it easy for the customer to buy. If you operate with the belief that it's not a question of whether a customer will buy additional products, but rather what a customer will buy, you generally will project this attitude to the customer—who will prove you right. You must condition yourself to be assuming. It is important, however, to pose your request for additional purchases in a way that will encourage a positive response. Consider these examples (immediately following the table on page 60):

Multiple Selling ($1 Average per Customer)

One sales associate

	Customers/Day		
	10	**20**	**30**
× $1	$ 10	$ 20	$ 30
× 5-day week	50	100	150
× 50 weeks	$2,500	$5,000	$7,500

Additional sales associates' sales (based on above figures)

Four	$10,000	$20,000	$30,000
Five	12,500	25,000	37,500
Six	15,000	30,000	45,000
Seven	17,500	35,000	52,500

Do you want the red earrings or the red-and-blue earrings to go with your new suit?

Would you like to have the regular or the large?

Would you like to have the belt or the tie?

By making it hard for customers to say no, you have in essence made it easy for them to agree to an additional purchase.

Your goal in multiple and suggestive selling is to sell, on the average, $1 more in product or service to each customer who walks through the door. Although some customers won't purchase any additional products, others will buy an extra $2, $5, or $20 worth of accessories.

It's easy to see from these figures that if each sales associate is able to sell an additional $1 to 10 customers daily during a five-day workweek, sales will increase significantly. These powerful statistics can work for you. Multiple or suggestive selling can make the difference between moderate success and great success. Believe it. In reality, the difference in sales between a number one, a number two, or a number three sales associate is generally a few dollars, not the thousands of dollars you are often led to believe.

Effective application of multiple and suggestive selling tools is the first step in achieving a 30 percent sales increase. As stated earlier, for example purposes a $25 average sale is used. Make adjustments to fit your actual sales average. If your average sale is $50, your goal is $2 per customer. If your average sale is $100, it is $4 per customer. If your average sale is $12.50, then your goal is $.50 per customer. Remember, ask every customer for additional sales, be prepared, motivate the customer to buy those accessories, and make it easy for the customer to say yes.

CUSTOMER OBJECTIONS

Why do customers say no? Is it because they don't like your products and services—the color isn't right, the size doesn't fit, the style doesn't suit them? Sometimes these are the reasons for a negative response. But you will usually find that customers use objections to slow down the selling process. Customers aren't necessarily saying they don't want to buy; instead, they are saying they need to think about their spending.

Objections are not sales stoppers, they are sales starters. Salespeople really don't begin to sell until the customer says no or gives an objection. Until that point, all you're really doing is providing information through presenting product knowledge, concepts, and opinions. Expect to hear objections. If you don't, then something is wrong. If a customer never challenges the quality or the price, you may find you're not working with a very serious buyer.

You have all heard the common objections:

I can't afford it.

I need to think about it.

Can you hold it?

I was just looking.

I'll have to bring in my husband (wife).

It's not the right color.

It's not American made.

I can buy it cheaper somewhere else.

When is it going on sale?

Today you are faced with two types of customer objections: true and false. True objections are the hardest to respond to because they are valid. Customers may state they can't afford the purchase, or perhaps the quality really doesn't measure up to their standards. False objections are easier to deal with because they're basically tactics used to slow things down. The customers are really saying they need more information before making a buying decision. Examples may be Can you hold it for an hour? or Let me think about it. Treat each objection as if it were true.

Sometimes statements are confused with objections. Comments from the customer such as, Collectible gift items are really expensive, or, The colors are really wild this year, are simply statements. Don't try to respond to a statement as if it were an objection. You will come across as someone trying to defend your products or services, your company, your prices, and, most important, yourself. Treat statements from the customer as a conversation.

The number one objection heard today is related to money. It can be disguised in the form of other objections, such as Can you hold it? or I have to bring in my wife (husband) or When is it going on sale? The customer may be embarrassed to admit it all boils down to money, and it's much easier to camouflage that fact with Let me think about it or I was just looking.

At some point you have probably had the opportunity to sell to a customer without encountering any objections. It was one of those days when you could have sold snow to people living in Alaska. Some food for thought: if you never receive an objection from the customer, you haven't asked for enough money. Again, we're asking you to break old molds and reshape old habits.

How would you respond if you spent several minutes with a customer who had asked a number of questions, examined the merchandise, and then suddenly said, "I was really just looking around." Would you simply thank them for stopping by, invite them to return, or hand them a businesscard? In some instances, these responses may be appropriate. As salespeople, you're the only ones who can assess the situation and arrive at the best course of action. In most instances, however, it is best to stay in the sale just one more time. Break the mold of giving up after the first objection.

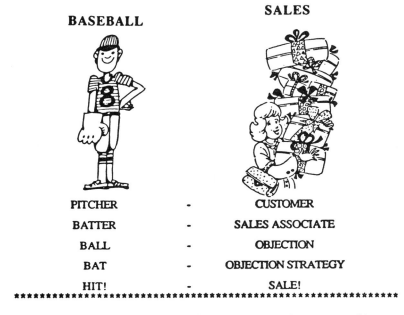

BASEBALL		SALES
PITCHER	-	CUSTOMER
BATTER	-	SALES ASSOCIATE
BALL	-	OBJECTION
BAT	-	OBJECTION STRATEGY
HIT!	-	SALE!

Let's examine the game of sales versus the game of baseball. In sales you work hard for success. However, success is broken into parts. The first part, the overall success of the store, is influenced by the image the store projects. Products or services offered, sales associates, advertising messages, product knowledge presentation, and so on all play a role in image. If your store's image isn't conducive to drawing customers, you can't move the customer into buying—the second part of success.

In the game of baseball, players also work very hard for success. In baseball, success is broken into two parts as well. Players play their positions in the field and work hard to get three outs so they have the opportunity to make hits and runs. In baseball, as in sales, you work at covering every position to achieve success. In the game of baseball, they can't make it to part two, hits and runs, if they can't get the outs and move up to bat.

To achieve the second part of success in selling, getting the customer to buy, you must do the same as players would in baseball. As in hits and runs, it all comes down to a one-on-one performance. In selling, it is the sales associate and the customer. While you're not going to sell every customer and answer every objection, you must try. In baseball, it's the batter against the pitcher. Players know they're not going to get a hit or a home run every time they go to bat, but they try. Professional ballplayers say, "To strike out is not good, but to stand there and watch the ball go by is far worse." If you're going to strike out, you'd better strike out swinging.

We all remember the great Babe Ruth, a baseball star from the past. We're told he struck out nearly four times more often than he hit a home run or a base hit. But what is he remembered for, his home runs and hits or his strikeouts?

In selling, professional sales associates say, "To not make a sale is OK, but to stand there and not try is far worse." So, if you're going to miss the sale, you'd better miss the sale by trying.

The key element is *trying*. You can't do anything until you try. When the customer says I'm just looking or Can you hold this, take the first step and break the mold. Try to stay in the sale just one more time by uncovering the objection, adding more value, and trying to close again. You'll surprise yourself with the number of sales you make when you stay in the game just a little bit longer.

Let's gain a thorough understanding of the objection strategy. It's a short, five-step process that helps uncover and overcome customer objections, provide logical answers, and add value that convinces the customer to buy your products or services.

The Objection Strategy

1. Smile Smiling conveys confidence! Practice in front of a mirror and perfect a confident smile. Smiling also helps a customer relax as you continue with the sales presentation.

2. Listen It's easy to stick both feet in your mouth when you start to talk too soon. Listen until the customer stops talking—and by all means, never interrupt.

3. Cushion A cushioning statement shows customers that you are listening, that you understand, and that you empathize with them. Cushioning statements may be as follows:

I understand how you feel.

Thank you for bringing that up.

I used to feel that way myself.

Many people (men/women) feel that way.

It's all right.

That's a good point.

You have a right to be concerned.

4. Restate Restating the objection serves two purposes. First, it shows you were listening. Second, it clarifies the exact point, giving you direction and allowing you to avoid any misunderstanding or misconceptions. Restating the objection may sound like this: So, what you're saying is ____. Is that right?

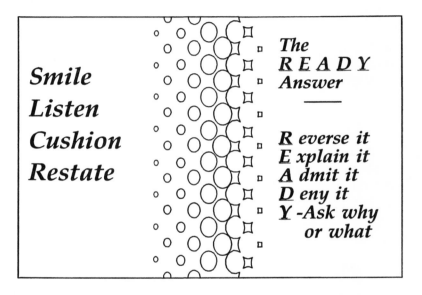

Smile
Listen
Cushion
Restate

The
R E A D Y
Answer
____

R everse it
E xplain it
A dmit it
D eny it
Y -Ask why
       or what

5. Use one of the READY answers The READY answers will help you stay in the sale, add more value, clarify, or expand the customer's knowledge. READY answers are:

Reverse it Reverse the objection in such a way that customers will have a greater understanding of its impact on, perhaps, their jobs, their homes, their families.

Explain it Explain or reexplain the store policy, returns and exchanges procedures, or product/service features and benefits. You will find this is one of the most frequently used READY answers you can add to your selling arsenal.

Admit it Don't try to hide the truth. If what the customer objects to is the truth, such as The quality just isn't in the product, and it really isn't, admit it. Then, requalify the customer from there and perhaps move him to a different product or service. This gives you direction.

Deny it   If the customer says something that isn't true, deny but defend it, and be ready to back up your defense. Often these objections come in the form of secondhand information, such as I heard this from my sister's cousin's uncle who lives next door to my best friend. If it is not true, deny it. But remember, it is important to be prepared to back up your denial with hard evidence.

Y—Ask why or what   Asking why or what is the most effective reaction because it places the responsibility of confirmation back on the customer. Ask them to explain why they don't like the product or service or what it is they don't like about the product or service. In many cases, you will find that customers will answer their own objections.

Objections

The following scripts are representative of the objections often heard in retailing today. Keep in mind these scripts are guidelines you can adapt to fit your situation.

Objection 1—Can you hold it?

Customer: Can you hold this for an hour/day?
Associate: 1. Smile.
          2. Listen.
          3. Cushion—It's all right.
          4. Restate—So, what you're saying is that you would like to look around before committing to buy. Is that right? (Phrase your question in such a way as to ensure the customer gives a yes answer—confirmation.)

Customer: Yes.
Associate: 5. READY answer E—Explain it: One thing
our store prides itself on is our return
and exchange policy. We recommend
that you write a check or put the purchase on your credit card, and take this
item with you as you shop around. This
way, you'll have the item right there to
make comparisons. You won't have to
remember details or run back and forth
to compare. And, if you decide against
our item, simply return it for an exchange or a full refund. Would you like
to do that?

Customers must then respond either yes or no. They
may decide to buy the item, or they may refuse. The point
is that you tried—break the mold! With a few changes in
wording, this answer will also work with those customers
who say they need approval from their wife or husband.
Statistics tell us that when customers make a purchase, they
generally stop looking around.

Objection 2—I want to think about it

Customer: Well, I'd better think about it.
Associate: 1. Smile.
2. Listen.
3. Cushion—I understand how you feel.
4. Restate—So, what you're saying is that
you just want to think about this before
you commit to buy. Is that right? (Make
the customer say yes.)

Customer: Yes.
Associate: 5. READY answer Y—Ask why or what:
Just to clarify my thinking, what exactly
did you want to think about? Was it the
color? The style? The shape? The size?

The price? (Always leave price for the
very last. Nine out of 10 objections today
are related to price.)

Whatever you do, don't give customers the opportunity
to respond before you provide a list of options. Provide the
information for them! Pause for a moment between each
option to receive a response from the customer. If you give
her a chance, she will stop and tell us the reason she's not
buying. The objection, I want to think about it, is too general
and must be broken down to find the real reason behind
her reluctance to buy. Once you have the real reason, you
can react accordingly—continue with the sale or stop.

Objection 3—It costs too much money

Customer: It's nice, but it costs too much money.
Associate: 1. Smile.
2. Listen.
3. Cushion—Thank you for bringing that
   up.
4. Restate—So, what you're saying is you
   really don't think it's worth the money.
   Is that right??? (Flavor your voice with
   lots of question marks as you say this.)
   This objection is a tough one. There
   could be several hidden meanings. The
   customer could really be saying I can't
   afford it or I don't see price versus value
   or It's just more than I wanted to spend.
   You may have to fish for the real reason.
   You can only get customers to say yes
   when you are equipped with the real
   reason for their objection.
Associate: 5. READY answer based on actual response.
   A (if the customer is really saying he
   can't afford it)—Admit it: I can understand exactly what you're saying. Let me

> show you something else (move cus-
> tomer to another product).
> **E** (if the customer is saying he doesn't see
> price versus value)—Explain it: You know,
> for me selling is so exciting that I some-
> times get ahead of myself and forget to
> explain about the product! Did I tell you
> about . . . (go through features and bene-
> fits to rebuild value versus price—remem-
> ber, the customer will never buy the prod-
> uct or service unless value equals price).

If the customer responds It's more than I wanted to spend, you are faced with a challenge. Some salespeople feel very comfortable with coming out and asking custom-ers, How much did you want to spend? or What price range did you have in mind? In most instances, this will lead customers down the path you want them to take. They will give you the extra information you need to move them into other products and services. However, asking how much a customer intends to spend can be offensive. Be sensitive to your customer and to the standard practices in your part of the country.

Objection 4—It's not American made

Customer: I wanted to buy an American-made product.
Associate: 1. Smile.
              2. Listen.
              3. Cushion—Many people feel that way.
              4. Restate—So, what you're saying is that if
                 you could find an American-made item
                 that is exactly like this one, you would
                 buy it. Is that right? (Make the customer
                 say yes.)
Customer: Yes.
Associate: 5. READY answer R—Reverse it: It would
                 be great if everything we purchased was

American made. We probably wouldn't
have high unemployment, interest rates
would be lower, and American businesses would flourish. The fact is, we
can't offer strictly American-made products. Sometimes we find just the right
foreign-made product to fit the needs and
desires of our customers, so we make the
sacrifice to meet their demand. But our
company is American, and even though
the product is foreign, you still help an
American company expand and create
jobs for Americans by purchasing goods
and services at our store. It's your decision, but this is the item you wanted,
isn't it?

At this point, allow the customer to talk. Sometimes she
will buy, and sometimes she won't. Be careful here and
avoid making your soapbox too big when you're standing
up there explaining things. Allow the customer to make a
decision based upon her own conclusions, not yours.

Objection 5—I can buy it cheaper

Customer: I can buy it cheaper at a discount store.
Associate: 1. Smile.
2. Listen.
3. Cushion—I understand what you're
saying.
4. Restate—So, what you're saying is if I
could sell you this exact item for the
same price as the discount store, you
would buy it. Is that right? (Make the
customer say yes.)
Customer: Yes.
Associate: READY answer E—Explain it: At this point,
build a conversation based on your company,

its benefits, the products and services you offer that discount stores don't. Emphasize customer service policies, refunds, exchanges, and all the things the store has to offer. Examine every benefit the customer receives at your store, as opposed to the discount store.

Objection 6—It's not what I wanted

Customer: It's just not what I wanted.
Associate: 1. Smile.
2. Listen
3. Cushion—It's all right.
4. Restate—So, what you're saying is that if we had the exact product that you wanted, you would be able to buy it. Is that right? (Make the customer say yes.)

Customer: Yes.
Associate: 5. READY answer R—Reverse it: Go back through the features and benefits of the product he is looking at, item by item, attempting to stay in the sale a little longer. Look at the color, style, shape, and price points again. Enable the customer to tell you exactly what he doesn't like. The product he wants may not even be available, but stay with the sale and determine whether it is possible to sell to him.

Objection 7—When is it going on sale?

Customer: When is it going on sale?
Associate: 1. Smile.
2. Listen.
3. Cushion—Many people ask that.

Associate: 4. Restate—So, what you're saying is that you would buy this item today if it were on sale. Is that right? (Make the customer say yes.)

Customer: Yes.

Associate: 5. READY answer E—Explain it: Right now, you have the opportunity to buy this product. You see it's the right color, right size, right style—you like everything about it. Even though it is full price today, you'll be getting exactly what you want right now. I don't really know when or if it is going on sale. It may be weeks or months. The home office controls our sales events. The problem you're faced with is that if you wait for it to go on sale, we may no longer have your size or the color and style. That's the risk you take by waiting for a sale. Today, you could take this product home and enjoy it. You don't have to wait and wonder if you can purchase it when it's on sale. Which would be better for you?

At this point, customers will respond. Let them talk. Not every customer will be sold, but many will make a purchase. For those who choose to wait, get their names and phone numbers to notify them when the product is on sale.

It's possible to go through an entire objection strategy two, three, four, or more times with a customer—but don't get carried away to the point that you are perceived as badgering the customer into buying. Remember, you spend many minutes building a relationship of trust with customers and letting them lead you into making the sale.

Don't sabotage your efforts by becoming pushy. You, the sales associate, must be able to determine how much is too much. It's your judgment call as to when to stop the objection strategy.

The most important aspect of successfully countering and answering objections is practicing your responses until they come naturally. There won't be time to check your notes or run through things in your mind when you're face-to-face with a customer objection. You must be quick, accurate, and convincing; otherwise, the customer is out the door before you've had a chance to work through the five-step process for overcoming objections. Be relaxed and know your answers before you need them. This will take practice!

Make a list of every objection you hear today. Enlist the help of fellow sales associates if necessary. Use a three-ring binder to keep your list together with your scripted responses. Create a textbook of responses that will enhance your chance of success in overcoming customer objections. An outline for you to use for this purpose follows:

Objection: _____

Customer:

Associate: 1. Smile
              2. Listen
              3. Cushion
              4. Restate—So, what you're saying is _____

_____. Is that right? (Make the customer say yes.)

Customer: Yes.

Associate: 5. READY answer: _____

_____

_____

In conclusion, being able to overcome the customer's objections is your second goal for your 30 percent sales increase. Your specific goal is to stay in the sale and overcome the objections of just one more customer per day. Again, you may find yourself staying in the sale two, three, four, or five times. You may find yourself responding to different objections, but stay in the sale. But if after one try you feel that the customer is not going to buy, then back away from the situation. As always, go down swinging. Don't allow the customer to give you objections and then walk out the door without at least trying to respond.

CLOSING SALES

Closing sales is the black-and-white process of success or failure. We're told there is very little gray area. In fact, many careers have been made or broken based on this process. Train yourself to stop thinking that if customers buy it means success and if they don't buy it means failure. Closing a customer is a success/success situation. If customers buy, you have achieved your sales success. However, if customers don't buy, you have succeeded in acquiring knowledge by asking them to buy and learning from their response. You must always strive to learn from your experiences.

Hundreds (perhaps thousands) of books, magazines, and articles are available to show you the world's best closing methods. Many times these sources claim to have the magic formula. We don't make this claim. The choice of a closing method is a very individual thing. You must be able to assess the situation and apply the technique most appropriate and comfortable for you.

The one practice that has the greatest impact is to condition yourself to ask every customer to buy. All they can say is no, and that one word can't destroy you. There's been a time in your career when you thought the sale was lost, but it was saved when you asked the customer to buy. Choosing the proper closing method is really easy—the

hard part is applying it when working with a real live customer. Observe customers' buying signals; through one of
the two standard buying signals (verbal and visual) they
will always tell you when they are ready to buy.

Verbal Buying Signals

1. The customer stops listening and starts to talk:

   Tell me again about that remote control.

   When could it be altered?

   Can you ship it?

   Do you have a box?

   What credit cards do you accept?
2. The customer starts expressing her intent to buy by
   telling you how she plans to use the product or service. You can see her starting to get excited.
3. The customer will start to justify ownership with
   logic versus emotion. She will begin to talk herself
   into buying. It's like watching a split personality at
   work. First she isn't going to buy, and then she
   starts to convince herself that she is going to buy
   your products or services.

Visual Buying Signals

These signals are sometimes more difficult to recognize because you are dealing with body language and facial expressions:

If the customer is smiling, it can be a signal of confidence—unless, of course, it is a corner smile with a
raised eyebrow. A full smile shows the customer is
relaxed and not threatened by what you're saying.

The customer may be nodding his head up and down or

giving a simple nod of acknowledgment and agreement with statements that you have made.

The customer may be reexamining the products—touching, reading the labels and care instructions, looking for minor flaws. In essence, he is verifying his choice and ensuring himself that this is what he wants.

A sure sign is the customer looking for money—finding the proper cash, looking at his checkbook balance, searching for credit cards. This is a definite sign he is ready to buy.

Closes

Watch customers. They will tell you when to close the sale. The closes we will discuss in the following pages may be known by other means. Most of these are universal to the world of selling, whether retail, insurance, real estate, computers, or any other product or service. We truly are creatures of habit. First we form habits, and then habits form us. We have all developed a favorite way of doing things. Although this is not necessarily wrong, it is important to diversify. An old standby close may not work in a certain circumstance. Develop, understand, and use as many closes as you possibly can!

In the first chapter of this book, we discussed the game of golf and how much easier it would be to play with all of the available clubs. Closing sales is similar. If you rely on one technique, you can play one round, but you won't enjoy it much. However, if you use different techniques to meet the demands of varied situations, you will enjoy the game much more and increase your chances of success. Learn and develop as many closing techniques as you possibly can.

1. Alternate choice close Some call this the alternate advance, yes-yes, or positive question close. This is, by far, the most frequently used close because it is precise and to the point. It requires nothing more than offering the customer choices that all end in the same result—the customer making a purchase!

Will this be cash, charge, or check?

Would you like the engraving in script or block?

Would you like to pick this up on Wednesday or Thursday?

2. Porcupine close   This is also called the stupid question or tie-down close. A customer has been looking at a particular product and begins giving buying signals in the form of questions. She asks, Does this come in blue? or Can you gift wrap this? Many salespeople respond with a simple yes. This is a response, not a close! Other salespeople go in for the kill with responses like If I could get this in blue, would you buy it? or If I could gift wrap it, would you buy it? This borders on being pushy. Professional salespeople will choose words carefully, remembering to lead, not push, the customer. They achieve this by asking the customer, Do you want it in blue? or Do you want it gift wrapped? These stupid questions are ways to lead the customer into telling you what they want. Let the customer lead into the close.

3. Costs too much close   This is also called the reduction to ridiculous close. You've all seen this close used on national television. For less than the price of a cup of coffee, we can sponsor a needy child in a Third World country. For only $88 per month, we can own a super combination radio/ fingernail file. For three measly installments, we can get our favorite magazine and receive lots of bonus prizes! This close is easy, but you must know two things:

How much did the customer plan on spending?

How long does the customer intend to use the product?

Once you know these two things, all you need is quick math. If an item costs $100 and the customer wanted to spend $80, you know the item is $20 too much. If the customer tells you he plans to use the item for two years, you can use this knowledge in the following way:

> $20 too much divided by two years of use equals $10 per year. Divide this by 12 to determine the monthly cost, which comes to $.83 per month. Divide the monthly cost by four weeks per month, and you have $.21 per week. Then divide the weekly cost by seven days to find the monthly excess cost of $.03 per day.

Reduce it to the ridiculous! The close may sound something like Is three cents per day too much to spend on an item you really want? Once you have broken the cost down to its lowest form, customers will usually feel ridiculous for having even brought up the price difference.

This concept will not always work—the item may still cost too much money. Stay in the sale by moving customers to a similar product in their price range.

4. Express doubt close   This is also called the erroneous conclusion or the false statement close. By expressing doubt in the customer's judgment, you may be walking on shaky ground. However, this close is effective if used at the right time in the right situation. You will typically want to use this approach when the customer seems to be sold on the product but can't seem to commit to buying. Express doubt regarding one or more trivial points about the product. For example:

> You are a shoe salesperson working with a customer who is a perfect size nine. You both know the size is perfect, but the customer just can't seem to make the final decision. You express doubt by saying, You know, that looks a bit tight on your foot. Stand up and walk a few steps. Hopefully, he will then defend his choice, assuring both you and himself that the shoe is perfect—and he will take it. Of course, the

danger in this approach is that customers may agree with you. If that occurs, take your lead from the customers' response and move them in another direction.

5. The balance sheet close This is also called the Ben Franklin or the positive/negative close. It works well with customers who can't seem to say yes. It shows customers all the positives and lets them fill in the negatives.

Positive	*Negative*
• Perfect color	_____
• Right size	_____
• Return/exchange policy	_____
• Guaranteed satisfaction	_____
• _____	_____

This process can be done on paper as a visual aid for the customer. The actual close may sound something like, ''The late Ben Franklin would use a process of positives versus negatives whenever he was confronted with a decision. On the positive side of ownership, we have _____, _____, and _____. What negatives do you see?'' (The secret to success when using this close is to let the customer point out the negatives while making sure the positives outweigh the negatives.) ''As you can see, the positives of ownership outweigh the negatives. Now, will this be cash, check, or charge?''

6. Negative desire close The concept of this close is simple. Tell people they don't want a particular item, and they will want it even more. This works well with customers who are set in their ways—opinionated on price, features, quality, and so on. They know exactly what they want! Such a customer may enter a store to buy a VCR with a remote and two-head features and may tell you exactly what they want in a VCR. You may have the perfect product in the price range, go through an entire sales presentation, and then have the customer refuse to commit. Switch directions!

Begin by telling them they don't need a machine like the one you are showing them—they really need one with more features, like the one over there. They will quickly justify purchasing the original product and buy it on the spot. The harder you try to switch their loyalty to another product, the more convinced they will become that they want the original product they looked at. If the switch doesn't work, they may end up buying the second product. Either way, you make the sale.

7. The story close This is also called the customer motivator close. It basically creates customer desire. To effectively use this close, you must know everything about the customer and the intended use of your product or service. What you're doing is creating a word picture that projects future ownership and use. The word picture will start off with Just imagine . . . or Picture this . . . These closes are similar to the word pictures we created when discussing desire to buy and multiple and suggestive selling.

8. The assumptive close This is also called the attitude close. The interesting thing about this one is that you really don't have to do anything. You are assuming the customer is going to buy. We've all been told that to *assume* only makes an *ass* out of *u* and *me*. This can be a dangerous close to use. However, you should work on the assumption that the customer is going to buy; that assumption will generally lead to use of the alternate choice close.

9. My dear old mother close This close is cute if used in the right situation. It is designed to work specifically for sales associates who just can't keep silent after closing. However, we recommend using it sparingly and as a last resort. For example:

You've been working with a customer and have closed with
Will that be cash or charge? The silence begins . . . 10 seconds . . . 25 seconds . . . If someone doesn't talk, you're
going to explode!

When silence has gone beyond the breaking point, use
the my dear old mother close. Put a big smile on your
face and show confidence when making this statement:
My dear old mother once told me that silence means
consent. Was she right? Then, wait silently for the customer's response. If you do this with a smile on your face
and in your voice, and you are sincere, the customer will
usually return the smile, begin to chuckle, or nod in
agreement. If they don't do anything immediately, go to
the cash register and start ringing up the sale. This is
guaranteed to provoke a reaction, which is just what you
need! Stay silent as long as you can and use my dear old
mother only as a last resort.

Silence is golden—remember these words! Many experts suggest the silent close. It is not really a closing
method, but the necessary second part of every close.
Once you have asked the customer to buy, you should
shut up! You have been taught, and learned through
experience, that the first person to talk loses. If the salesperson is the first to talk, pressure is taken off the customer. Although it is difficult, the real test in a good close
is to remain silent and wait for the customer to respond.
Even if customers speak first by saying no, you are still
in the sale because you can continue to lead them based
on their response. Remaining silent is a talent that must
be developed over time. It can and must be done if you
expect to be a successful closer.

You have probably noticed that these closes are connected and interchangeable. You may use two or more on
the same customer, and it may take a number of closes
before the sale is actually made. For example:

Sales associate: Will that be cash or charge?
Customer: It's too much money.

You respond with the costs too much close. The customer changes directions and asks for a different product. You then move to the porcupine close. Then, you might return to the alternate choice close and finish with my dear old mother.

In this situation, you have used five different closes. You must know and apply as many closes as possible and be prepared for any situation.

Create your own closing book using a three-ring binder. Develop the closing techniques we have reviewed and include others you have learned from your experience. Practice your closings so you will be relaxed and confident in different selling environments.

Once again, don't badger the customer; know when to back off. You are not going to close every sale. Some days, you will close sales with every customer. Other days, you won't be able to give your products or services away. That's what happens in the world of selling. Remain flexible and adapt gracefully to every situation.

Your goal in closing customers is to close one additional customer each day. Use a closing method on a customer whom you would have normally allowed to object and walk away.

IN CONCLUSION

The three areas we have covered—multiple selling, overcoming objections, and closing sales—give you many sales opportunities. In the beginning of this chapter, we made some bold statements. We said that you would have the opportunity to increase your personal sales by 30 percent. Let's look at how you can achieve this by utilizing the three concepts we have discussed.

Current status

Average sale	$25	
Customers per day	20	
Customers sold	8	(40%)
Total sales per day	$200	
Total week (5-day)	$1,000	
Total year	$50,000	

Multiple selling (Goal—$1 per customer)

Average multiple	$1	
Customers	8	
Sales per day	$8	
Total week (5-day)	$40	
Total year	$2,000	increase

Overcoming objections (Goal—sell just one more customer)

Average sale	$25	
Customers	1	
Sales per day (+ multiple)	$26	
Total week (5-day)	$130	
Total year	$6,500	increase

Closing sales (Goal—sell just one more customer)

Average sale	$25	
Customers	1	
Sales per day (+ multiple)	$26	
Total week (5-day)	$130	
Total year	$6,500	increase

Current	$50,000
Increases	$15,000
% Increase	30%

These are tangible numbers and small averages. Look at the intangibles. How many of these sales will be new customers, and how many times in the next year will they return to your store? How many new friends will you have developed? And how many of these new customers will refer business to you? How much more impressive will these numbers be if every sales associate in the store accomplishes these simple goals?

Earlier, we discussed the two schools of thought. It would be easy to try to spend millions of dollars in marketing, but it would be difficult to justify the expense. To become truly great at your profession as a retail salesperson, you must develop yourself using things you have to work with. If your current close ratio is 3 out of 10, by increasing your closing ratio to 4 out of 10, or 5 out of 10, you will generate an additional 10 percent to 50 percent in sales simply by doing what you do best—leading the customer into buying.

Don't expect to master all of these areas overnight. Practice, practice, practice! The key is to know and use these concepts for your benefit. Share this information with others on your staff so everyone can contribute to your store's success. Everyone will enjoy the final result!

Chapter Three

Environmental Attitude

INTRODUCTION

I n this chapter, we will concentrate on the concepts and attitudes of a complete store environment. In most instances, the areas we will address will not show instant, immediate results that can be registered on the cash register right now. Rather, this chapter will emphasize long-term growth.

Balance your sales efforts. In the selling world, you must have a balanced existence. You will do some things to gain immediate results, including special sales promotions, inventory reduction sales, or other promotional and marketing events. Typically, these immediate result/short-range efforts are designed to make the cash register ring right now.

Some actions we take ensure medium-range results. These include merchandising changes to reflect the seasons or perhaps bringing in new products to meet consumer demands and buying trends.

Finally, certain things can be done to ensure long-range results. These include implementing customer service programs, using opportunities, and changing or enhancing the attitudes and actions that you possess and practice in your stores every day.

Attitude and action—this is the perception you give the customer about yourself and your store. It's the visual look you present. It shows the customer your store and its associates, products, and services. It's seizing the opportunity given by the customer to create new services and programs. It's listening and communicating. It's all in how and what you project to the customer, positive or negative.

Hundreds of outside influences could control attitudes and the perceptions passed on to the customer. These may include:

- Home office policy.
- Receiving the wrong merchandise.
- Personal problems.
- Customer problems.
- Associate problems.

Success and a positive outlook are journeys, not final destinations. When we're confronted with a situation or opportunity, it's human nature to immediately respond in a negative manner. However, many sales associates never get past the negatives to see the positives. How often do you respond in these ways with regard to a new opportunity or situation? It sounds like a good idea, but

The home office will never approve it.

I can't afford the postage.

We don't have time to fill response cards.

Our sales staff won't be motivated.

It is a good practice to weigh the negatives and positives of an opportunity before jumping right in. Be realistic and objective in the first analysis. But then, be prepared to move past the negatives and assess the positives as well. A final action or judgment should never be made without looking at a situation from all angles. Determine the feasibility and potential benefit versus the associated costs and expenses—then take appropriate action.

VISUAL MERCHANDISING

Visual merchandising is perceived in different ways by different people. It might be:

- *Physical displays*—in the windows, in the actual store, on back walls, on side walls, or actual display props you use.
- *Product*—the clothing, shoes, jewelry, leather goods, cameras, or gift items.
- *Manner of display*—the racks, tables, shelving, props, and grids used to display products and services.

Many people never go beyond these elements when it comes to visual merchandising. They tend to think only of the displays, products/services, or manner of display, without considering the concept at its basic level—the look of the store, its associates, and product/service displays. We will look at each element.

The Store's "Look"

When thinking of visuals, you usually think of actual displays. Let's take this concept a step further and consider the look of the entire store. Simply stated, the store must reflect the lifestyle you want to project. If the lifestyle of your store and its products and services is very leisurely, then the look should be equally casual and leisurely. On the other hand, if the lifestyle is very formal, then that should be reflected throughout the store.

Although it would be nice to have an unlimited budget for altering the look of your store, you can make improvements and changes inexpensively and effectively. The key to this concept is cleanliness. The store must be clean from top to bottom. Carpet, windows, counters, cases, racks, shelves—everything must be clean! If it's broken, don't use it. If it's dirty, clean it. Keep a constant eye on your store with regard to cleanliness. Make the store look sharp!

There is a problem encountered by every sales associate. You see your store every day and become accustomed to the dinginess, dustiness, and dirtiness. Your perception of the store is very different from the customers'. They view everything from a different perspective, and you can believe they see everything—good or bad. Try to put yourself in the customers' shoes and look at your store through their eyes. What changes need to be made? Is a positive impression being made? Are you making an effective statement about your store's lifestyle?

The Associates' "Look"

We've all heard of the wonderful book, series of tapes, and updated versions of *Dress for Success*. The most popular combination of clothing continues to be blue or gray pin-striped suits, white long-sleeved shirts, and red or colorful power ties. This advice is good for executive-level professions, or if your store targets that type of lifestyle. However, keep in mind that your manner of dress is a direct reflection on your store's lifestyle target. A suit or other conservative business attire may not be most effective or appropriate in all store environments.

Common sense is your best guide when it comes to your look. We're not advocating a drastic change in wardrobe or a uniform approach. Rather, we suggest you take your cues from the store and its lifestyle projection. A customer's perception is altered and disturbed if your look is radically opposed to that of the store. If you look out of place, then you will be perceived as such. Never out of place, however, are cleanliness and good grooming. Insist that these be your standards.

Consider a situation that we addressed several years ago.

> A store manager asked us to stop by his store to help him solve a problem. He indicated that his store did great business all day, but suddenly died off around 5 PM. We arrived at the store at 4:30 PM; as we'd been told, the store was very busy. Customers were coming in and out, the cash register was ringing, shoppers were shopping. A few minutes before 5, a very large man walked out of the back room and up to the lot line, and then stood there with folded arms. At first, we thought he was waiting for someone in the store. But we were wrong; he was a member of the night shift. Standing six feet six inches tall and weighing around 250 pounds, this fellow was intimidating. Although he was a gentle giant, you sure couldn't tell by his demeanor or appearance. If customers ventured into the store, he followed them. Of course, traffic diminished in his awesome presence. After an hour of observation, we moved Mr. Night Shift away from the lot line. Booming business suddenly returned.

Be careful as you position yourself in the store. We realize this sounds like a broken record, but keep yourself busy. A busy environment creates an air of excitement—something is going on inside your business. We know many managers who rearrange their stores on a weekly or bi-weekly basis. Everything in front goes to the back, everything in back goes to the front. Often, these same managers will unpack new merchandise in full view of customers, which gives customers the opportunity to see the store in a new and exciting way. Many times these managers take old merchandise off shelves and racks, place it in boxes, and make it appear as though they're unpacking new merchandise.

In any event, try to stay away from the lot line. It gives the appearance that you are waiting for a bus.

The Product's "Look"

The look you present to customers will often determine whether they choose to enter your store or walk on by. Ask yourself how often a customer has come into the store in the past week and asked to see a specific product or service that was displayed in a front window, back wall, or front door.

Time is the most critical product placement consideration for stores in shopping centers and malls. On the average, a customer can walk from storefront to storefront in just eight seconds. That is the time you have to make a positive visual impression that will entice the customer to enter your store. During those eight seconds, you must also compete with outside distractions. Customers may be distracted by:

* Children who are misbehaving.
* Activities in the mall or other stores.
* Dodging other customers walking by.
* Conversations with friends.

Do you strive to make the visual looks of your products and services appeal to existing customers or attract new customers? Displays function as opinion molders and lifestyle indicators, and they are a valuable part of the sales process. They also introduce new products and services and change customers' preconceived opinions of existing products or services. Concentrate on reaching the broadest segment of the consumer market through using innovative visual displays that make a positive and strong impact on your total look.

CREATIVITY

Dare to be different! Creativity is an essential ingredient in attracting the customer. Many of you don't have control over your store's looks. Often, your company provides everything you need for the displays, including grids, props, and instructions, in order to create a standardized look among its stores that will trigger instant recognition. For those of you who do have control over this element, creativity can boost your efforts tremendously.

Rather than fall into the same old habits and techniques, stretch your imagination and design unique methods for displaying standard fare. Allow customers to see a traditional product or service in a new light, thereby changing their buying opinions and creating action! Don't settle for ease or convenience when developing a merchandising display program. Instead, position merchandise in a different way, use a variety of materials and methods, and set a buying-oriented tone in your store.

We all do it. We drive the exact same route to and from work, day in and day out. The first few times we make the trip, we notice everything—the locations of the gas station, grocery store, office complexes, and new construction. After a period of time, things become a blur, and we fail to notice changes we encounter each day. The day comes when we pull into the parking lot, get out of the car, shake our head, and wonder, How did I get here? Because the trip is so automatic, we don't even have to concentrate on it!

Customers do the same thing when shopping. They walk by the same stores, often taking the same route through the center. They are on automatic pilot and fail to notice anything new or different along the way. Although the products or services you offer may differ from those of your competitors, your look is so similar that customers sometimes fail to notice that your store exists. In fact, many managers have complained that shoppers will enter their store and ask how long they have been in the center, thinking the store is new. This occurs even though the store has been a tenant for years! The moral of this story is to create a visual impact that attracts customers. Your look must generate attention. Does it?

As we've said before, visual displays are opinion molders and lifestyle indicators that enable you to attempt to change the customer's point of view. You may try to display the newest and best products but end up disappointed when they don't take off in a sales boom. The critical element to the success of even your most innovative displays is the creation of a mental vision or image showing the customer ownership and use of your products or services.

We have had the opportunity to view the following visual displays created by retailers just like you. Take a moment to read them carefully; notice the elements of creativity that effectively brought them to life.

> A department store display was placed in front of a main entrance to a shopping center. It displayed boxer shorts and tank top undergarments for young girls. A mannequin had been dressed in the ensemble and positioned lounging on top of a pile of throw pillows with a telephone receiver in her hand. School books and other youth paraphernalia were scattered around to indicate she had just come home from school. The scene created a casual, typical teenage atmosphere. We had the opportunity to stand nearby and watch customer reactions to the display. Almost every woman who walked by said, ''That looks just like . . .'' with a smile on her face. A mental picture had been created because the department store had brought the display to life by giving it personality.

> A cosmetics store designed a display of products and services centered around a life-sized poster of Marilyn Monroe. In the window was placed a small director's chair, a spilled box of popcorn was on the floor, ''streamers'' of old movie

film were hung from the ceiling, and confetti was strewn around. Its cosmetic products were prominently displayed throughout the scene. Hardly a customer walked by without getting involved in the visual picture. The store had creatively set the stage.

A waterbed store with no windows chose to set up a display at the front of the store. Mannequins were dressed in pajamas. The woman was propped up against pillows and reading a newspaper, with a breakfast tray in front of her. The man stood behind the bed. As people passed by the store, many took a double look just to assure themselves these were mannequins and not real people. Customers definitely noticed this display!

A jewelry store created a display featuring diamond solitaire engagement rings in a small front window case. A deck of playing cards was displayed to represent a game of solitaire. Scattered around and throughout the cards were very simple diamond solitaire engagement rings. The display reinforced the store's promotion and capitalized on the cleverness of word association.

It is easy to be so caught up in your products and services that you forget or neglect to use innovative materials and methods to create visual displays. Borrow or otherwise acquire additional props to present a complete picture. In this way, you create a visual image of ownership in the customer's mind. The following are some popular items to use in creating your visual looks:

1. *Posters and pictures*—borrow these items from an art store, print gallery, or movie theater in your area. Movie posters are often disposed of, so you might be able to obtain them for free.

2. *Furniture items*—large pieces (dressers, chests, sofas, or chairs) are not needed to be effective. Try small

items (end tables, lamps, patio furnishings, plants, and small chairs) to add personality to your overall look.

3. *Sporting goods*—every season "sports" at least one popular athletic event. Use your imagination and play up to these big-time attractions. An example of using sporting goods in an unlikely environment was demonstrated by a jewelry store. Although jewelry store displays are typically restricted in size, tennis bracelets were effectively presented to the buying public with the help of bright orange-and-yellow tennis balls. Various bracelets were draped over and around the balls to attract attention.

4. *Jewelry items*—use earrings, bracelets, watches, or gold chains to accessorize your look. Other stores will usually permit you to borrow this merchandise if your store doesn't carry them. This technique was effectively utilized by a ladies' clothing store in a display of accessory watches. A mannequin wearing a trenchcoat and hat, and looking very mysterious, was placed in a front window. The coat was pinned open, with a variety of watches hanging on the coat's inside lining. A sign saying Ya Wanna Buy a Watch? was strategically placed by the mannequin. The store had received over 500 of these watches in October in preparation for the Christmas selling season. It had to reorder twice before Thanksgiving!

Ask yourself the following questions as you build your next visual look of products and services:

1. How and where can the customer use this product?

2. Is it an old, new, or rejuvenated product?

3. Is it a gift item, or will it be purchased for personal use?

4. What type of lifestyle and/or use does the product reflect, and are you going to attempt to change the customer's point of view?

Creativity is the key! This factor brings an ordinary display or visual look to life. Because customer habits die hard, it may take time to achieve the desired change. They may not be expecting you to change, to become creative. Give them time to notice and accept the new you. Continue your efforts to breathe new life into your visual displays—it will pay off.

A long-lived argument exists regarding frequency of display changes. At the very least, create different visual looks when there is a change in products or services or their use or with the change of seasons. According to your time limits, it is also a good idea to change the display and spot-lighted products and services every 30 days or every two weeks, if possible. The more often you exhibit creativity and give customers something new to notice, the more often they will make a positive buying decision. As you show customers new lifestyles, opinions, or products and services, they will begin to change their perception of your store.

Unless you are fortunate enough to have a large staff and a diversity of grids, props, and accessories to build your visual looks, you may have to borrow from other stores. Most stores are usually willing to lend some of their supplies. In return, you can provide a small sign in the display crediting your borrowing source.

The staffing needs for creating and changing displays on a regular basis can be provided by local schools and colleges. Many have students who would love to gain experience and exhibit their artistic merchandising talents. You may be able to find this service free of charge in exchange for giving the student a good job recommendation.

Take every opportunity to be innovative, creating visual looks that promote your products and services in a new and different way!

CUSTOMER SERVICE

An easy definition of *customer service* is everything that you and your store do to affect customers and their attitudes toward you. Customer service creates customer loyalty. However, customer loyalty is nothing more than the absence of something better. Customer service must always be seen through the customers' eyes, not yours.

Success or Failure

The national corporate sales meeting was just about over. The only award remaining was the prestigious Store of the Year trophy. The corporate president explained the standards used to judge the stores and their performance. First, percentages were used so everyone had an equal chance. Second, the stores were rated on total sales, sales per square foot, sales per hour, increases over previous year, mystery shopper reports, and profits. The banquet room became dark except for a single spotlight on the president and podium. The occupants of the room eagerly awaited the president's announcement of the winner. He slowly opened the envelope, building everyone's excitement and anticipation higher. The president finally read the name of the winning store and manager. The room exploded with applause for the colleague who had won the ultimate award.

When the room finally became quiet, the president asked the manager of the Store of the Year to say a few words. The manager began to speak:

I'm sure many of you are wondering how our store achieved its performance. Did we have special merchandise that no one else had? No—we had the same products your store does. Did we have a great location? No—our location is the same as yours. Did we have less competition? No—we have as many competitors as you do. Did our store have special sales and promotions? No—many of you are in better markets. Did our store have better salespeople? No—on average, they are all about the same. So then how did our store win this award if we are all about the same? I can sum it up in two words—*customer service*. In short, we have created an image and environment that enable the customer to perceive us as the best. In their eyes, we stand above the crowd. We give our customers reasons to shop and buy and to return to our store again and again.

The winning manager then held the trophy high in the air and repeated the words *customer service*. The room exploded in applause as everyone gathered around the winner.

Later, after the other managers had gone, one remained. This lone rookie store manager walked up to the winner and offered warm congratulations. He asked her to explain the concept of customer service in more depth. Smiling, the winner offered a seat to the new manager and said, Take some notes if you wish. Customer service is:

Balance Your Operation

In the retail business world, you must have a balance of efforts and existence. First, you do things to gain immediate results, such as special promotional sales events, inventory reduction sales, or other short-term marketing events. Typically, these short-term/immediate result efforts last only a few days or a week. They are designed to make the cash register ring now!

Second, you act to ensure medium-range results through seasonal merchandising changes or the introduction of new products in response to consumer demand and buying trends.

Third, you create ideas to ensure long-range results, such as implementing customer service programs, creating opportunities, and projecting positive attitudes and actions in your store.

Unfortunately, most businesses never get past the immediate and medium-range activities. For most, it's easy to forget long-range activities because they don't often show tangible results. For example, have you ever had a customer come up to you and say that the reason he spends money at your store is because you provide gift boxes? Chances are you haven't.

Short-term/immediate result activities and medium-range activities will generally take care of themselves. They are the basis for your current success. However, the long-range activities and their details create the great successes in your future!

The positive side to balancing your operation is that most of your competitors are not concentrating on long-range efforts and details either. This gives you a great opportunity to step forward and be first.

The bottom line of long-range results is that it takes strong customer service programs, effective use of opportunities, and positive attitudes and actions to create customer loyalty. Your primary goal, both now and in the long run, is for the customer to continue to choose your store. Actually, customer loyalty is nothing more than absence of something better. It is up to you to ensure that you give them every reason to consider your store the best of the bunch! Remember, it's details that make the biggest difference in how the customer perceives you and your business.

Attitude and Action

Hundreds of books, magazine articles, memos, and daily conversations have driven the words *customer service* deep into your professional life. If you have good customer service practices, you have success. If you don't, you could fail. Sadly, many businesspeople are driven by the fear of failure rather than the joy of success. Which of the two following situations best describes your attitude?

Fear of Failure?

The Joy of Success

1. You, the salesperson, wait until customers ask for something or request information to complete their buying decision before you offer to assist.
2. You, the salesperson, willingly offer something or volunteer information to customers without first being asked.

Situation 1 is driven by fear: if you don't give customers what they ask for, you could fail. Situation 2 is driven by joy: if you offer customers everything and then some up front, you should succeed.

Your attitude and actions create customers' perceptions of both you and your store. Are your attitudes and actions positive or negative? With customers, there is seldom a gray area.

Dozens of influences, both internal and external, could control the attitudes and actions you project to the customer. These may include:

- Home office policy.
- Receiving wrong or outdated merchandise.
- Personal problems.
- Customer problems.
- Associate problems.

Is it possible to always be positive? Reality tells us it's not. However, you must get past the negatives and analyze the positives. A final attitude or action should never be determined without looking at the situation from all angles. For example, a salesperson is overloaded with customer complaints concerning a certain supplier of products and finds it difficult to express a positive attitude when angry customers make product returns and request refunds. It becomes so bad, the salesperson feels like running and hiding every time she sees a customer walk through the door—whether the customer is making a return or not. This then has a negative effect on the entire store.

On the other hand, if the salesperson accepts the challenge to create a positive customer when confronted by a negative one, things may turn out differently. The salesperson could return to the store's records to find sales receipts or layaway receipts, anything that may identify customers who purchased the problem supplier's products. The salesperson could then contact each customer who may be affected by the problem merchandise, inform them of the problem, and invite them to return to the store to resolve any complaints. The customer would then perceive the store and its staff in a positive light, minimizing negative responses.

The first scenario illustrates the devastating effect a salesperson driven by fear can have on the store. The second shows the positive influences that result when a salesperson is driven by the joy of success.

Opportunity

Have you ever let an opportunity pass you by because of fear of the unknown or just as a matter of habit? Here is a story about someone who did:

> An aspiring young lawyer was trying to hail a cab in New York for the first time, without much success. As a taxi approached, the lawyer stepped forward, sure he would be picked up. But the cab stopped 10 feet in front of him and picked up a distinguished-looking gentleman. The lawyer threw up his hands in despair just as the cab pulled up beside him. The driver yelled, "Hey, kid, my passenger wants to know if you want to share this cab!" The young lawyer, unwilling to take a chance, declined the invitation. Moments later, another cabbie picked him up and said, "Sure wish I had gotten that fare right before you! I heard on the cab radio that it was F. Lee Bailey!"

Do you open the door of opportunity when you have the chance? Opportunities will come in many different forms. Whether opportunities are great or small, it is up to you to find and seize them!

If you listen closely to customers, they will tell you everything you need to know. They give you the opportunity. Then, it is up to you to become driven by the joy of success and offer your specials to the customer. For example, if a customer tells you she intends to give her purchase as a gift, where is the opportunity? It could be your return and exchange policy—the fact that no sale is final. It could be providing a gift box or gift wrapping—convenience for the shopper. It could be offering to ship the package—conveying cost and time savings for the customer. It could be any number of things!

The catch to opportunities is in your willingness to tell

customers what you have to offer. It doesn't mean a thing unless they know about it! Listen to customers—they will give you the opportunity you are looking for. Tell them about it!

Logic and Common Sense

As you look at each opportunity, follow the five points of customer service found in logic and common sense. In short, investigate things and determine if and when a special service or program should be offered.

1. Listen and act   All too often, we come up with a great idea and human nature convinces us to act on it immediately and then listen. In the retail market, customers will tell you everything that is important to them. All you have to do is listen first, and then act. Be careful! Many times the things you feel are important are not important to the customer. A special service must be seen as important through the eyes of the customer.

There was a shopping center located in the middle of a baby-boom area. The center's first reaction was to supply more strollers to accommodate parents while shopping. It spent hundreds of dollars on new baby strollers. Yet, after several months, the strollers were just gathering dust. The shopping center found that parents brought their own strollers. What customers indicated a need for, however, was diaper-changing stations in the restrooms. The shopping center found out later that parents would bring their own strollers and shop until the babies' diapers needed changing, then return home. Perhaps the center could have responded to the real need by listening first and then reacting.

2. Keep it simple   Customers need their complex lifestyles simplified! For some reason, our society has a desire for complexities. We feel things must be complicated to be successful. However, any store program you develop must be simple to succeed. People will be afraid to participate in a complex or confusing program. Sometimes customers will become angry with you for attempting to add to the already overwhelming complexity in their lives.

For example, a store runs a half-price sale, which is a form of customer service designed to offer customers the opportunity to save money. When the customer first sees the sign publicizing the sale, that's all he wants to see. Matters are complicated by making it necessary to read the fine print to understand the full nature of the sale. True, the store does have a half-price sale, but the customer must purchase one item at full price to receive the second item of equal or lesser value at half-price. If the customer has not read the fine print and finds out at the cash register that he has not met all the conditions to qualify for the sale price, he will very likely feel angry and taken advantage of. The message —keep it simple! In this particular example, half-price is actually only a 25 percent discount. It makes more sense, by marketing standards, to advertise a half-price sale. This catches the customer's eye, but communication is vital in minimizing complexities! Remember, if something can be misunderstood, it will be!

3. Make it genuine People want things they can depend on! If customers can't depend on your business and its "special items," they will find a place where they can— even if it means driving farther or spending more money. Once again, customer service creates customer loyalty, which is actually nothing more than the absence of something better. Look at the automobile industry in the early 1980s. American consumers felt they couldn't depend on the cars produced by US manufacturers. Their answer— purchase foreign automobiles. Why? They perceived greater dependability from foreign cars and were willing to pay more. Always remember, the consumer has a choice! This "consumer's choice," as long as you have competition, will remain a very strong purchasing factor.

If customers can't depend on you for your special order timetable, they will find someone who can.

If customers can't depend on you for a positive return and exchange policy, they will find someone who can.

If customers can't depend on you for availability of items, they will find someone who can.

If customers can't depend on you for follow-up to their problems and concerns, they will find someone who can.

If customers can't depend on you for your layaway system, they will find someone who can.

And so on . . . through the customers' eyes!

4. Results Be careful of expected results on long-range projects, such as customer service. Don't get caught up in the short-range/medium-range result trap. Often you can't measure a customer service project or opportunity with any standard other than a customer's smile. If you have listened, acted, kept it simple (communicating when necessary), made it genuine, and found your sales increasing, you must assume it's working. You should never assume anything, and, in essence, you haven't. If you have completed all preliminary work, you've done all you can do, and the results will be the judge of your effectiveness. If you really want to test a customer service program or opportunity, do the following:

> Take an existing item and change it so it is no longer advantageous to the customer, and see what happens. For example, if the store offers gift boxes or gift-wrapping services to the customer, take it away. If the customers' smiles disappear, you've got a problem. Many stores find it helpful to periodically ask their customers for their opinions of various

service items, such as layaway or cash refunding. Remember, customers will tell you everything that is important to them—if you just listen!

5. Stick with it   The world is made of four groups:

- People who make things happen—an elite group of performers.
- People who watch things happen—most fit into this category.
- People who wonder what happened—just lack of experience.
- People who have no idea what happened—watch out!

The magic of the groups is that you can decide in which one you fit! If you decide to be a person who makes things happen, you must live by that decision, which includes taking responsibility for the good, the bad, and the ugly. It's easy to say, I want to be a person who makes things happen, but actually doing it is often not as easy as it sounds. It requires commitment.

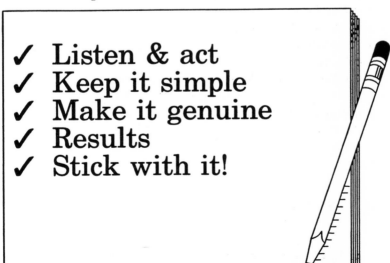

✓ **Listen & act**
✓ **Keep it simple**
✓ **Make it genuine**
✓ **Results**
✓ **Stick with it!**

Projects

You've heard the saying You can't please all of the people all of the time. You'd better believe it, or you'll drive yourself crazy trying! To satisfy everyone in your market, you may need to promote hundreds of special services. Even if you have that many services to promote, you will still never completely satisfy your market. Why? Because you'll be scattering your efforts too widely for any one of them to be truly effective.

Athletic coaches often use the saying Give me 120 percent of your effort. If you were capable of giving even 100 percent all of the time, you would burn out and lose control. Instead, commit to giving 80 percent and remaining in control at all times. This is not suggesting that you should do less than your best. Know your limitations and focus your attention on giving your absolute best to the absolute most you can do. It's far better to offer only a few special services and offer them with excellence than to offer dozens with mediocrity.

Start with your store's existing special services, which include all short-range and medium-range efforts such as return and exchange policies, special orders, layaway, and gift certificates. Put your house in order and then, as the need (as indicated by customers) arises, add additional special items or services to satisfy them. Remember, they will tell you everything you need to know!

The winning manager then turned to the inquiring rookie, who had listened intently to the secrets of success, and said,

> That, my friend, is customer service! In the last 15 minutes, I've given you everything you need to get started. Remember, I said *get started*. The rest is up to you! You may not be on stage next year to accept the award for Store of the Year; it will take time to perfect the skills necessary to implement and maintain a successful customer service system. Over-

night success cannot be expected. There will be months and years of adjustment, change, and trial and error. Success is a journey, not a destination. I spent seven years as a manager before reaching the top. And, I'd be wiling to bet that very few actual sales dollars separated the top 10 contenders for the award and that even fewer separated me from the number two manager. Those dollars represent only an extra customer or two a year. It's amazing what customer satisfaction can really mean. Well, our company's new sales year started two weeks ago. I've got to go—there's a lot of work to do. I'll see you next year!

Researchers have concluded that if, after five years of operation, a business is generating at least 60 percent of its sales from repeat customers, it will continue to succeed. If the business is only generating 30 percent of sales from repeat customers after those five years, it won't see its 10th year!

How long does it take to build a business? Days, weeks, months, or years? In most cases, it will take many years of hard work to build a strong foundation. But it may only take a few weeks or months to destroy it. That is a sobering reality.

The obvious details of customer service are simple. You start by helping the customer make the right buying decision:

- You're friendly and courteous.
- You satisfy customers' needs and wants, and make them feel good about their purchases.
- You may offer to gift wrap the item.
- You may have a layaway system for convenience.
- You may accept credit cards so they can enjoy purchasing now and paying on time.
- You may offer to ship the item to another location.
- You may have in-house credit for easy purchasing power.

- You may offer liberal return and exchange policies.
- You may have national buying power and national locations.

In basic terms, you help customers through the sale. If they leave happy, you have increased the probability that they will return. And we know that repeat business is good business!

LOOK TO THE FUTURE

Don't view one sale as the happy ending to the story. See it as a challenge to continue bringing that customer back to the store again and again to purchase your products and services. The following areas of customer service have been labeled The Standard Five. These areas may be oldies, but they are goodies! They serve their purpose well by increasing the probability of repeat customers.

1. Preferred Customer Lists

Some of the more popular uses of a preferred customer list include:

- Special sales events.
- New product intro.
- New line intro.
- New store openings.
- Catalog mailings.
- Yearly sales events.
- New personnel intro.
- New service intro.
- Awards and honors.
- Private sales.

A preferred customer list is worth its weight in gold!

Average sale	$25
Customer itch cycle	3 times/year
Sales per year	$75
20 years' total sales	$1,500
Times 3,000 customers	$4,500,000

If your store's average sale is $25, and your average customer makes an average purchase three times per year, that equals $75 in total sales. Over the next 20 years, that customer is worth $1,500 in total sales. Multiply that times only 3,000 customers, and you have created $4.5 million in sales for a yearly average of $225,000. That's impressive!

If the store's total sales for the year are $900,000, and you add that extra $225,000 from the use of preferred customer lists, you have achieved a 25 percent sales increase! Even though this example is a perfect number situation, it happens every day in someone's store. Is it yours?

This customer service technique is so vitally important, every customer should be asked to sign up for your preferred customer list. It's too easy to simply place a box on the counter stating Sign Up For Preferred Customer Mailing List, hoping passively that customers will comply. They probably won't. For this tactic to be an effective advertising tool, you must train yourself to personally ask the customer to sign up, regardless of whether a purchase is being made. If you feel uncomfortable approaching customers directly and soliciting mailing information for this purpose, simply get a customer's name and add the relevant data from the check, charge slip, or phone book. The very least you should do is get the customer's name.

A certain percentage of customers will always refuse to sign up for the preferred customer list. They don't want to be on another mailing list and receive more junk mail. Consider using the following response:

I would hate to have you show up in our store the day after a big sale or event only to find out you had missed it. Our special events are often advertised only to preferred customers. Many times, you can save from 20 percent to 50 percent or more. If I can notify you of upcoming sales, you then have the opportunity to decide whether you would like to take advantage of the sale. At least you know in advance about upcoming events that may interest you. Now, what was your name and address?

2. *Customer Profile Cards*

Customer profile cards will help eliminate guesswork. Some businesses can make good use of this system, while others are not greatly affected. Review the following, and see if it sounds familiar:

I have just entered your store to buy a gift for my wife. I know she shops at your store all the time because I see her bringing home shopping bags from your store. I'm in a dilemma because

- I don't know what her size is, but she's about this big and this tall.
- It's her birthday, so I need to take it home today.
- The last time I bought her a gift, it didn't go over too well. I bought her a gift certificate, and I'm still hearing about how impersonal that was.
- I really have to do a good job on this one!

How often do you encounter customers like this? Every day! It's frustrating for both the salesperson and the customer because neither is prepared to accomplish their goals. The salesperson can't sell, and the customer can't buy.

Customer profile cards help you focus on merchandise the customer wants or needs. They are useful in providing information about customers' preferences, sizes, colors, and other variables. All parties involved in the sale benefit from the use of customer profile cards. Customers are assisted in making appropriate buying decisions, fewer items are returned, and customer service is enhanced because the purchase has been simplified and the customer's needs met.

Customer profile cards should include the customer's name, address, telephone numbers, sizes, styles, color preferences, likes, and dislikes. You could also include brand names or whether the customer likes to purchase markdowns or hot-off-the-rack merchandise.

The next section of the card should contain the customer's purchase record, showing what was purchased and when. This record will identify purchasing patterns that will assist in making future sales. Such information is useful for announcing upcoming sales as enticements to buy and for recommending products/services that will coordinate with previous purchases.

Along with sharing customer profile cards with friends and relatives at gift-giving times, they are great tools for new sales associates. New associates are given a head start on sales with such a file by getting to know their customers.

Customers' purchasing histories are indicators of their itch cycle. This cycle is created by the customer, demonstrating a purchasing pattern that can be capitalized on. Check all customer profile cards regularly, every month or two, to find customers who have met or missed their unique pattern. When customers miss their itch cycle, it's time for a quick phone call to uncover a problem, correct a situation, or motivate them to stay with their purchasing pattern.

Customer profile cards are perfect for:

- New associates—immediate customer base.
- Birthdays.
- Anniversaries.
- Determining purchasing patterns.

— Customer Profile Card —

Name: _____ **Jennifer Welch** _____

Address: _____ **123 Main Street** _____

City: __**Urbandale**_____ State: __**IA**_____ ZIP: **50322** _____

Telephone: __**515-654-7332** _____

Work Phone: __**515-223-6900** _____

Sizes, Styles, Likes, Dislikes: ___**Likes bright colors and** _____

needs a size 7. Really likes "Esprit" label. _____

— Purchases —

Date: _____ **3/12/89** _____ Item: __**Dress & Top** _____

__**Floral print dress with dropped waist** _____

____**Style #A-37645** _____

___**"Esprit" green & blue top** _____

___**Style #F-21766** _____

---

3. *Thank You Cards and Letters*

If you gain nothing more from this chapter than a knowledge of the importance of sending thank you notes, your time has been well spent! A thank you note is an important extra that you can provide for the customer. It's very easy to automatically say thank you to customers, especially after you have just taken their money. However, take time to express your thanks outside of the selling environment. It is a sincere gesture of appreciation to which customers respond well.

We've all received thank you cards or letters from a business after making a purchase. It makes us feel special and even better about our purchase. It also reconfirms our loyalty and commitment to continue buying goods and services from that particular business. For that reason, we recommend that you send a thank you card or letter to every customer who makes a purchase. Don't set a minimum amount the customer must spend to receive a thank you card. If you do, you may leave out some very important people. The person who spends $25 today could be a $200 customer tomorrow. Your thank you note for the $25 purchase could be the catalyst that persuades this customer to continue shopping at your store. Investing in a stamp and postcard or letterhead is an inexpensive way to make a priceless impact!

Plain or fancy, typed or handwritten, thank you notes should work within the lifestyle your store presents to the customer. Preprinted messages or handwritten expressions of gratitude reflect your commitment to this integral standard of customer service. The only rule is to hand address each envelope for the crucial personal touch. Customers are more likely to open a handwritten envelope first. Be certain your spelling is correct and your writing is legible. Remember, you are creating a lasting, positive impression!

A story concerning a department store and thank you notes was recently shared with us. This department store decided to embark on a thank you program. Each customer making a purchase received a small personal message saying Thanks Again For Your Business! After a few months, an interesting thing occurred. The store began receiving thank you notes from the customers for sending them thank you notes! Another astounding thing happened. Some customers cut up competitors' credit cards and enclosed them with their thank yous, stating, "As long as you continue this practice, I will never shop anywhere else!"

Obviously, a thank you note is one of the most important customer service programs your store can implement. Some retailers even like to send discount coupons with their thank you notes, although we recommend you save these for other advertising efforts.

Dear Jim,

I just wanted to drop you a short note to say thanks for your purchase of the new digital stop watch. As you had said, you needed one that was going to be accurate within 1/100th of a second. I'm sure you will find the one you purchased will meet your needs just fine.

Good luck with your upcoming Track Season.

Thanks again.

Sincerely,
Susan Smith
ABC Company

✓ Once you start, don't stop
✓ Every customer, every sale
✓ Fancy or plain
✓ Handwritten
✓ Hand addressed

If doing handwritten thank you letters is not appropriate or is too time consuming for your business, another popular method is a follow-up phone call with each customer. These economical calls can be made during slow periods.

4. *Customer Newsletters*

Customer newsletters keep customers informed about your business and industry. They should be lighthearted yet informative. The real estate industry has perfected the newsletter concept. If we were to purchase a home through a real estate company, we would receive a newsletter for the next 12 months telling us all about home improvement ideas, landscaping, insurance, consumer watches, home repair scams, new products, and so on. The value of this newsletter, as well as our positive perception of the company, grows with each edition.

A newsletter produced by your store should contain information about the store and industry as well as nonbusiness-related data. Tell customers about upcoming sales, new product arrivals, store changes, new sales associates. Then add upbeat and entertaining trivia. Let the customer get to know you and the store's personality.

A word of advice—don't make your newsletter appear to be all advertising. We urge you to put in some extra touches that will help give the newsletter a longer shelf life. Your objective is to keep it in the hands of your customer for as long as possible. Make it entertaining with such popular inserts as:

- Recipes.
- Exercises.
- Vacation ideas.
- Personal care.
- Fashion updates.

- Health care tips.
- Movie reviews.
- Book reviews.
- Thoughts for the day.
- Household hints.

When gathering information for your newsletter, look for insights. Trade magazines are a good source, but company buyers are even better. They can tell you exactly where your store is headed both fashion- and industrywise. Utilize the insight of buyers, supervisors, and other key home office personnel when developing copy.

The newsletter need not be lengthy; one typed page will generally suffice. Or, if your handwriting is especially legible, consider that approach for a different look. Simply photocopy your finished form and then distribute it.

We recommend distributing the newsletter as a flier, giving it to customers at the point of sale, where it can be slipped into the bag after a purchase is made, or handing it to them as they enter or exit your store.

The frequency of publication will depend on your budget. Consider putting out an edition once a month, once a quarter, or with the change of seasons. A good rule is to publish your newsletter based on the customer's itch cycle. In this way, you are fortifying the cycle and perpetuating customer purchases.

How much will it cost to publish a newsletter? It all depends on frequency and whether you want to do the work yourself or use contract services. If you use your time and talent to write, type, and photocopy, it is very inexpensive. One thousand photocopies at five cents each is only $50. Or, you can spend several hundred dollars having it professionally written, designed, typeset, and printed. If you publish monthly, $200 per issue may be too expensive, whereas that may be reasonable for a quarterly publication.

5. *Customer Complaints and Problems*

Customer complaints and problems are ideal customer service opportunities! Since you may not agree with each of our recommendations or you may not be able to implement each one due to company policy, we have provided alternative situations.

We don't have control over the problems that can happen, only over our reaction to them. It would be great if you could just sell, sell, sell and never face a complaint or problem. But dealing with customer complaints and problems is a necessity in business. Since it is impossible to be all things to all people, don't try to be!

Certain customers will never be satisfied, regardless of how hard you try to please them. All you can do is offer everything within your power and company policies to make that customer happy. The three biggest complaints and problems expressed by customers are as follows:

A. Quality The products and services do not meet their expectations.

B. Sales associates The sales staff is uninformed or not authorized to make decisions. Common personnel-related complaints may include:

No one available to help at the register.

Unfriendly, discourteous, generally negative staff.

The attitude that they are doing the customer a favor.

No personal touch.

Endless waiting for assistance.

C. Store policy Customers lack an understanding or appreciation of store policies.

And, of course, customer complaints invariably come at the most inconvenient time—during peak hours, when the store is full of customers, or on the busiest day of the week. A customer with a complaint or problem is generally angry, loud, offensive, and demanding. Wouldn't it be wonderful if all customers coming into the store to complain could express their concerns nicely?

Consider this ideal scenario. A customer enters your store carrying a package. You know it's going to be a problem, return, or complaint. She starts by saying, "I just purchased this item three or four weeks ago. I've only used it three times, and it's already broken. I don't know if you can help me, but I can't use it like this. Is there anything you can do?" You would have the tendency to respond in the same nice manner if you were approached in such a way.

Customers are accustomed to venting their frustration to get results. They angrily say, "I only purchased this item a couple of weeks ago, and it's already broken! I only used it three times! What are you gonna do about it?" Customers have decided they must be loud, angry, offensive, and demanding to get their problems resolved.

It is important to remember that you don't have control over the problems, but you do have control over your reaction to them. Use the following as guidelines:

Don't take it personally   Although it is difficult to dissociate from verbal assault, you must try to depersonalize the customer's complaint. A loud, demanding customer is just looking for someone to be the scapegoat. You just happen to be the lucky one. Notice that we use the term *lucky* to describe your position—we'll discuss the opportunities your situation provides later.

It is natural to become defensive when you are the target of a customer's wrath. However, a defensive attitude only fuels the frustration level on both sides.

Smile   Don't flash a full, toothy smile, or you'll be perceived as a smart aleck. Instead, offer a genuine, small smile of understanding and concern. This shows confidence and will help offset and lighten the customer's angry attitude.

- Don't take it personally

- Smile

- Listen

- Disarm

- Restate

- Use an "R"
  Repair it
  Replace it
  Refund it

Listen   Listen to everything customers have to say without interrupting. Wait until they have finished before speaking. This shows respect and gives the impression that you consider their complaints important. An attentive listener disarms angry speakers, helps them relax, and prepares the speakers to be courteous when it is their turn to listen.

Disarm the customer   By expressing your understanding of their dilemmas, you eliminate their hostility. The following statements have the same effect as jumping over the sales counter, standing next to the customer, putting your arm around his shoulder, and saying:

- I understand how you feel.
- You have a right to be concerned.
- I've been in your spot before.

Restate the problem   This clears the air and ensures no misunderstanding of what the customer has communicated. It also shows the customer that you have been listening. Preface your restatement with, "If I understand you completely . . ." The customer may talk about unrelated things when expressing a complaint, so narrow it down.

Use one of the three *R*s   After restating the problem, offer the customer your assurance that you will help her:

- *R*epair it.
- *R*eplace it.
- *R*efund it.

You might say something like "We will do everything in our power to satisfy your interest in this matter. You have a choice of three things we can do. We can repair, replace, or refund. Which would you like us to do?" The important thing is to give the customer a choice and let her decide how you can satisfy her.

Some stores have a no refund policy, which makes it more difficult to satisfy the customer. Don't be afraid of refunds.

Customers may often choose to repair or replace an item, but they would like the choice of a refund as well. We are not trying to change your policy, but it has been our experience that stores that don't offer refunds are asking for trouble. Customers know how to get their money back one way or another. They make frequent calls to home offices, district managers, and owners. They contact the Better Business Bureau. They get television news reporters interested in their plight. They picket stores that don't give refunds. So, avoid confrontations and negative publicity by offering the choice of a refund, together with repair or replacement.

Have some fun with customer problems and complaints. You have an audience, so take advantage of it! It's like the old television commercial—"When E F Hutton talks, people listen." That's true in the retail store environment, where customers are listening intently to see how well your store handles complaints. This is the perfect opportunity to exhibit your commitment to customer service. Play to the crowd and make a lasting, positive impression with your customers.

Remember,

Don't take it personally.

Smile.

Listen.

Disarm the customer.

Restate the problem.

Offer one of the three Rs.

You'll recall our earlier statement that you are lucky when confronted with customer complaints or problems. There is no greater opportunity to enhance customer service than handling customer complaints or problems. Look for them, seek them out, and don't be afraid of resolving them. This is your chance to satisfy an unhappy customer and solidify or build customer loyalty. If customers are treated fairly and with respect when it comes to complaints, they will continue to do business with your store.

Customer satisfaction is based on the theory of the numbers 1–3–7. For every 1 customer that you satisfy, you'll be lucky if they tell 3 others about your store. But for every 1 customer who is dissatisfied, you'll be lucky if they tell only 7 others.

Studies indicate that you see only 15 to 20 percent of actual problems or complaints. The remaining 80 to 85 percent are never voiced to you. That's dangerous. If you are aware of a problem or complaint, you can resolve it. If you don't know about it, the results can be very damaging. Even though a customer doesn't tell you about a complaint, you can be sure they will tell someone else, painting a negative picture of your store to potential customers. Consult the customer profile cards to determine if an itch cycle has been missed. Contacting customers to inquire whether a problem exists can save their business and enhance your image in their eyes, as well as their friends' eyes.

Total customer service goes beyond the extras you do. It also encompasses those things you try not to do. Avoiding actions that anger or alienate customers is as important as performing actions that will please them. The key to this issue is your reaction to the customer. If something is important to the customer, it should also be important to you. For instance, if your customers feel thank you notes are important, this should be high on your list of priorities. Seize the opportunity!

Take your lead from your customers; they will present every opportunity you need to serve them well. When someone walks into your store to purchase a gift, go beyond the sale and serve them in other ways:

- Box or gift wrap the purchase.
- Begin a customer profile card.
- Send a thank you note.
- Offer layaway.
- Give them a newsletter.

This same customer, if served well, may frequent your store many more times in the next year—at Christmas, Valentine's Day, Easter, or just because. Remember, customer loyalty is built on customer service. Use the standard five when it comes to customer service. Building on the small details makes a big difference in the long term. To be effective, customer service programs must mesh with customer desires, needs, and wants. By looking through the customer's eyes, you can offer programs that are important to the customer. And, those are the only kind that count!

The Wheel of Success

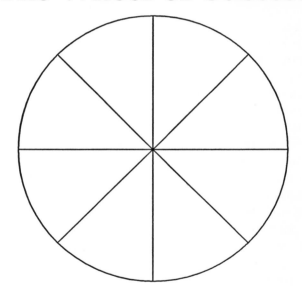

ADD TO THE WHEEL ...

- THE SALE
- CUSTOMER PROFILE CARDS
- CUSTOMER NEWSLETTERS
- LAYAWAY
- DELIVERY
- ALTERATIONS
- PHONE FOLLOW-UP
- GIFT WRAP
- GIFT CERTIFICATES

- PREFERRED CUSTOMER LISTS
- THANK YOU LETTERS
- COMPLAINTS
- IN STORE CHARGE
- SPECIAL ORDER
- BUYER PARTIES
- PERSONAL SHOPPING
- PURCHASE CLUBS
  (PUNCH CARDS)

We have all seen the television show "Wheel of Fortune." In selling and customer service, there is a Wheel of Success full of sales and opportunities to make more sales. If you rely only on the sale to generate more business and keep the customer coming back to your store, you land on bankrupt and get nothing. But if you look for and capitalize on customer service opportunities, you will advance your cause and be rewarded for your effort. You can spin the wheel and build repeat customers to ensure your ongoing success.

Things will constantly change. You must continually add to your customer service repertoire. Once you launch a customer service program, it is critical to stick with it as long as it is important to the customer. The keys are insight and consistency.

IN CONCLUSION

We would like to share with you some information from a book entitled *How to Win Customers and Keep Them for Life.* When customers or potential customers have contact with your store, they will experience certain consequences of their action. Their future behavior, whether they continue to do business with your store, depends largely on those consequences. The more customers feel rewarded, the greater the odds they will continue to be customers. The less customers feel rewarded, the greater the odds they will not repeat their behavior. They will become someone else's customers and spend their dollars elsewhere.

A humorous story illustrates this idea. Once upon a time, a farmer wanted to breed his three female pigs. He loaded the sows in the back of his pickup truck and took them to visit several boars at a nearby farm. While they were getting acquainted, the first farmer asked the second, "How will I know if my pigs are pregnant?" He responded, "That's easy, they wallow in the grass when it takes, and they wallow in the mud when it doesn't take.''

The next morning the farmer awoke, looked out his window, and found the pigs wallowing in the mud. So he loaded them into the truck and took them back to the boars. The following morning, the pigs were still wallowing in the mud. Undaunted, the farmer once again loaded the pigs in the truck and took them back to the boars for a third time, hoping for positive results.

The following morning, the farmer was away from the farm, so he anxiously phoned his wife and asked, ''Are they wallowing in the grass, or are they wallowing in the mud?'' His wife responded, ''Neither. Two of them are in the back of the pickup, and the third one is up front blowing the horn.''

There are two basic lessons in the story. First, every behavior has consequences. In the story, the female pigs visited the boars (the behavior) and liked it (the consequences). Two, future behavior depends largely on the consequences of past and present behavior. If the consequences are rewarding, the odds are great that the behavior will be repeated. The pigs' visit to the boars provided a very rewarding experience, and so they were eager to repeat it. To put it simply, you get more of the behavior you reward.

In the previous chapters, you were given many examples and opportunities to see the selling process up close. A New Beginning brought you back to the basics, but if you have ever experienced a selling slump, you know the only way out of a slump is to sell yourself out. A Dominating Position gave you an inside look at the three most important areas on which to concentrate if you want to improve—and improve dramatically by staying in the sale just one more time. Environmental Attitude concentrated on your selling posture and looking at the big picture.

Within your selling structure, seek new knowledge every chance you can. Unlike other professionals, retail salespeople are not required by law to update and refresh their skills. But common sense tells you it's a must for survival! Be careful of the fads and fashions of the time; they will come and go. Cornerstone basics will always remain the same. Finally, I ask you to share this book on selling with your associates. Help everyone in your organization be more successful. Don't put this material away. *Use it!*

PART

II

Management

Chapter Four
Essential Skills

INTRODUCTION

W hat is management? Some say it is to succeed by accomplishing tasks. Others say it is to achieve one's purpose. And a few say it is to manipulate others to do what you want. Often, the word *manipulation* brings on a negative feeling. Most people immediately picture a "villain"—an evil person tricking people to do things they otherwise wouldn't do. Don't be afraid to associate the word *manipulation* with management. The dictionary tells us manipulation is the art or skill of control. In its positive state, it is win–win. In its negative state, it is win–lose.

Hundreds of books have been written on the subject of management. Some tell us to be tough and rule with fear and intimidation. Others tell us to just play ball and don't rock the boat. The experts tell us there are four distinct characteristics of good managers:

- Manage with confidence, never fear.
- Use logic, never emotions.
- Set high goals, but never out of reach.
- Have persistence.

There are four distinct types of managers: (1) Managers who *make* things happen; an elite group; only 3 to 4 percent of all managers fit into this category. (2) Managers who *watch* things happen; most managers today fit into this group; it's human nature to observe and avoid the initial risk before the fact. (3) Managers who *wonder* what happened; these managers won't last long; thank goodness this group is small. (4) And finally, managers who *have no idea* anything happened at all; believe it or not, there are a few people in this group.

Rather than attempting to "point fingers" or to box you into a particular category, this material is designed to help you take action! Become a manager who makes things happen. Don't just manage by the seat of your pants. Know how and when to make decisions by understanding the elements, facts, and figures that affect your organization. These are essential skills.

Your first step in dispelling old habits and methods of management is to fully believe the following: You are a manager of everything in your environment—the store, merchandise, time schedules, policy applications, and so on, with the exception of people. You will *never* be able to manage people—so stop trying! However, you will *always* be able to lead people. You will find that over half of the problems associated with management won't exist anymore if you follow this principle. As you review this material, view yourself as the store leader, not the store manager, and see the difference.

CRISIS MANAGEMENT

Some managers believe if it's not broken, don't fix it. This philosophy is no longer OK. If it's not broken, *break it* must be your new battle cry. If not, you will continue to run to crisis to crisis to crisis—all of which take up your valuable time. It's uncanny, but in most crisis situations, we can look back after the fact and see ways the problem could have been prevented. Even more puzzling, the negative crisis experience does not motivate us to prevent it from happening again in the future. (For many, experience is the ability to recognize a mistake after we have made it again.)

Consider this situation: It's your day off. You have slept in late and are now ready to run a few errands—to the post office, bank, dry cleaners, grocery store, and then meet a friend for lunch downtown. You are driving around town and have just pulled onto the interstate when your car stops running. As you pull the car over to the side of the road, you discover you are out of gas (that big E on the gas gauge means *empty*, not *enough*). Now you walk to the nearest gas station, borrow a can of gas, walk back to the car, and then drive back to the station for a fill-up. Two hours of precious time have been wasted, and you missed your lunch date.

When people run out of gas (and they do!), they feel angry, stupid, aggravated, inconvenienced, and silly, and some even blame the car (this stupid car).

These same feelings can be related to management under the if-it's-not-broken-don't-fix-it philosophy. Simply stated, an ounce of prevention is worth a pound of crisis. Instead of focusing on the crisis itself, focus on preventive measures to control the crisis. If you want to avoid running out of gas, fill up when the tank is one-quarter full. As well, if you want to avoid not having enough staff for an upcoming sales blitz, arrange for additional associates before the event begins.

Become a mechanic. Often, we have to look beyond the surface to see a crisis brewing. Often a potential problem is hidden under the guise of normality, striking when we are least prepared. The key element is to ferret out problems (break things) before they become crisis situations. The following four-part system will enable you to evaluate (break things) within your environment.

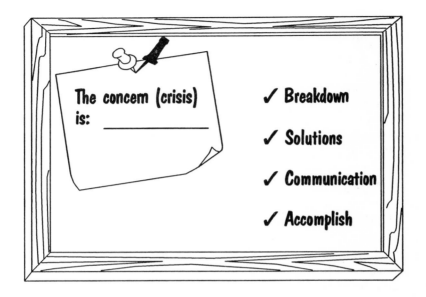

Breakdown

Look at every element of a concern from its most basic level to its most advanced. List each element and objectively assess its value as a strength or weakness. In most general terms, the strengths will not contribute to a problem or a potential problem. On the other hand, the weaknesses will cause the crisis to occur.

Solutions

Assess each element of concern (weaknesses) individually and from a variety of viewpoints. Strive to identify problem areas and move forward to change their status from weaknesses to strengths. Consider many options and don't limit yourself to a single solution or means of change.

Communication

This is where the solutions grow from the idea stage into practical application. The way to implement a solution or a means of change is to tell everyone involved what has been discovered and how they are affected. It is somehow seen as common for management to keep things from subordinate associates, choosing instead to form a secret society of management eyes and ears only. Although this may be appropriate at times, it is critical to communicate with everyone when it comes to crisis intervention and problem resolution, or the prevention thereof. By offering the *why* aspect of a course of action—communication—you equip your staff to be a part of the solution process. As always, incorporate their viewpoints. Communication is a two-way street. As a manager, you can learn something from your right-hand person or from the new associate.

Accomplishment

Are we convinced that a particular concern or potential concern is no longer a problem? Have we succeeded in turning every weakness into a strength? Although there are no guarantees, we can now move forward from a position of strength. Rather than being surprised by unforeseen dangers, we are prepared for contingencies. This preparation enhances our control over the many elements of the store.

This four-part system can be used with any facet of your operation. Break it! Once it is broken, you can rebuild it to see how it works. At first, this will seem like a long task. After you have completed the process many times, 15 to 20 minutes is all it will take (from start to finish) to get your concern down on paper. The following examples show the practical application of how the system works.

Concern   Upcoming sales event.

Breakdown

Advertising.	Merchandise.
Refreshments.	Sales staff.
Decor.	Tables.
Store hours.	Signs.
Flyers.	Details of event.

After considering these elements of the concern, we determine the following as weaknesses:

• Inadequate staffing for the event.

• Shortage of event signs.

• Details of the event and/or specific areas may be confusing to the consumer.

Solutions

• Recheck the schedule for existing associates and make changes where possible. If necessary, bring in outside associates.

• Contact home office or manufacturers for more signs. If unavailable, create your own.

• Prepare for a store meeting—ensure everyone understands the details. Talk through possible customer situations and questions and appropriate answers.

Communication   Conduct a store meeting or talk with each associate individually. Discuss the concern itself and the tactics you are taking to strengthen its success. Let everyone know what is expected of them with regard to the event. Post details of the event in the back room so no one is left out or has an excuse for not participating according to the plan.

Accomplishment   Delegate various projects to store associates. Get everyone involved! Keep a checklist, remain flexible, and be ready for anything.

Will the upcoming sales event take place without a crisis? It may or it may not, but much of the event's success will be determined by how well you broke it and rebuilt it.

Concern   Customer complaints/returns.

Breakdown

Products.

Associates.

Customers.

Store policy

Return time.

During the breakdown process of this concern, your goal is to find the unusual elements (i.e., Are the products of one supplier being returned more than others? Is one associate responsible for more returns than others?). During the breakdown process, we discover the following weaknesses:

- One associate has more returns/complaints than all others combined.
- Complaints/returns are most often geared toward quality (it didn't last).

Solutions

- Look closely at the associate: Are his returns proportionate to sales? Is the associate overselling customers on quality—telling them more than is true?
- In general terms, are the associates overselling the product's quality?

Retraining—education of the associates—may be necessary to not oversell the products and services. And develop a system of tracking the complaints and returns to create a graph or chart for future reference.

Communication   Conduct a store meeting or talk with the associates individually. Discuss the concern itself and the tactics you are proposing to lower the store's return ratio. Let everyone know what is expected of them.

Accomplishment   In this example, time will tell. If the return/complaint ratio is falling to acceptable levels (goals), your plan is working. If not, remain flexible and ready to make changes in the solutions.

Will the complaints/returns ratio be lowered from your efforts? It may or it may not, but much of your success in addressing this concern will be determined by how well you broke it and rebuilt it.

Concern   Assistant manager is promoted to a store manager position. (Your righthand person is leaving.)

Breakdown   Loss of a key person—her sales, abilities, leadership, and her reflection on your training and developing her for the new position. During the breakdown process of this upcoming event, you find the following weaknesses:

- The other associates have not been developed to help take over duties and responsibilities of the promoted associate.
- You have not determined who will be promoted into the position of assistant manager or whether you will bring in someone from outside your store to fill the position.
- The store may go through a transition period, which may disrupt attitudes, motivation, sales, and many other interconnected elements.

Solutions

- Immediately assess the remaining associates and determine their abilities as a group to take over duties and responsibilities, including sales, opening and closing, and scheduling.

- Complete or reassess your existing associate development plan to have your associates ready to take over other positions during associates' absences.
- Settle the issue of promoting or bringing in an outside person to take over as assistant manager as soon as possible.
- Prepare for a store meeting to talk about the transition period.

Communication   Hold a store meeting, talk with the associates individually, or talk to them during the going-away party for your assistant manager. Discuss your concerns and the tactics you are proposing to make the transition go as smoothly as possible.

Accomplishment   In this example, be ready for anything! Flexibility will be your key to success. The remaining associates will be learning new duties and working different hours, personality conflicts could occur, and many other challenges will face you.

Will the transition go as planned? It may or it may not, but much of this concern will be alleviated by the abilities of the remaining staff, their adaptability to change, and how well you broke it and rebuilt it.

It is human nature to concentrate on things after the fact, not before. For the most part, you will find yourself using this four-part system to examine what went wrong rather than applying crisis prevention. For this, the system works perfectly. However, when you examine areas of your store that look good on the surface, many times you will uncover minor weaknesses. If these weaknesses are treated now, they may never turn into crises.

As you have no doubt noticed, the three previous system application examples all had one thing in common: they are all controllable from your environment. Often, you will have no control over many crisis situations. You can't control shipping delays, associates who call in sick five minutes before their shifts, a sudden blizzard, walk-in customer complaints, or home office policy, just to name a few. However, if at all possible, use this system to control what you can.

Prevention of crisis situations will assist you in many areas: lower stress, better time management, more motivation, and more production for your company. Remember, if everything is going great, don't worry—it won't last! If it's not broken, break it.

DELEGATION

Wasted personnel is a major problem facing retail management today. The stores are full of good people who are ready, willing, and able to contribute, if we just let them. Welcome to my store, I built it, I know everything, I can do everything. Now the fun begins. You have severely crippled your staff and created supermanager. Rather than speaking in terms of *I, me, mine,* and *my* with regard to the store, begin using the magic word *we.* By substituting the word *we* in these instances, we create a team environment where cooperative effort gets the job done. Each member of the team has special talents to contribute—let them! Working together, we will succeed!

One of the best-kept business secrets is a manager who delegates. Do you like to delegate? Would you like to delegate more? The main reason managers don't like to delegate is because the final outcome is not what was planned. If a job/duty/task is not completed the way we expect, we find ourselves saying or thinking, Next time, I'll do it myself.

The Ivory soap percentage (99.44 percent) of delegating problems involves communication, or the lack of it. Delegators must communicate clearly with a delegatee so there is no misunderstanding of the job/duty/task and the method or manner it is to be performed to achieve the desired result.

You can use the following five-part system to elevate your delegation techniques and enhance their outcome. All five parts must be present and incorporated into delegating, or you will continue to say Next time, I'll do it myself!

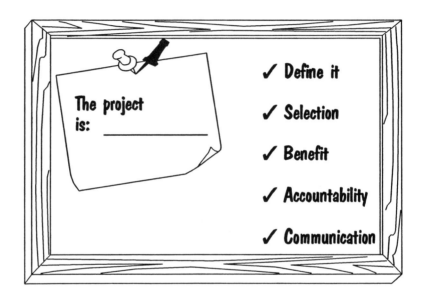

1. Definition

Define the job/duty/task in as much detail as possible. The finer the definition, the easier it will be to complete. In most instances, it's best to overexplain and leave nothing to chance.

2. Selection

Select the appropriate associate to complete the job/duty/task. Determine if the job is part of a training program; if so, the associate-in-training should do it. If the task is routine, perhaps a rotating schedule is more appropriate.

3. Results and Benefits

The associate who receives the delegated job must see a benefit for herself or she will withhold her best effort. This holds true whether the task is simple or complex. Show the associate how she can benefit from completing the job. Having seen that the job is desirable, important, and rewarding, she will put her best foot forward. Self-interest is always a prerequisite to delegating.

4. Accountability

Do you expect your associates to be accountable for their actions? They should be—they must be! How will you judge their performance with regard to the delegated task? First, there must be an approval/nonapproval factor. Let them know what is expected. Second, you must respect the golden rule of accountability—only one person is accountable to another. It defeats the purpose when two or three people try to assist; confusion reigns. And finally, inform the associate of the whos, whats, whens, wheres, and whys involved.

5. Communication

Communication constitutes the most critical aspect of delegation. When you find yourself saying Next time, I'll do it myself, trace the problem of delegation and you will discover that the culprit is the lack of communication. Communication involves a complex series of events, as was outlined in Chapters 1 and 2.

The communication of a delegated job is a double-edged sword. On one side, managers feel they are at a disadvantage. They tell of explaining the job to a T. Still the job is not completed as desired. The associates will seldom admit a lack of understanding. Instead they will nod their heads yes but not have the foggiest idea what their manager is talking about. The manager may find herself communicating the task two or three times before it is completely understood. The phrase ''The third time's the charm'' could have been coined with delegating in mind.

On the other side of the sword, associates feel they are at a disadvantage. They tell of managers who try to explain things but leave out little details. Managers know how to do the job very well and have done it so well, it's second nature to them. Most times it's not second nature to the associate.

Never assume there is one best way to communicate to all of your associates. Different personalities require different styles and methods of communication. And different skill levels require different details. One associate may need precise instructions, while another may only need a brief direction. Utilize various methods of written and spoken communication with your associates.

Several years ago, the popular method of delegation was to throw jobs at associates and allow them to learn by trial and error—a baptism-by-fire theory. Unfortunately, when you subject your associates to this method of communication, the learning usually ends up in more error than success. Critical areas include:

1. Define the job.
2. Select the associate.
3. Benefits and results.
4. Require accountability.
5. Communication.

The following examples will show the practical application of the delegating system.

Job   Weekly markdowns.

Definition   Mark down the price of merchandise, and change the tickets to reflect the change using the computer printout as the guide and checklist. Don't forget window and wall displays, and note what items may be on hold or layaway in case they are returned to stock.

Selection   Select someone who is accurate and detail oriented, someone who knows the merchandise well or the associate in training.

Results and benefits   (1) More sale merchandise, resulting in more store sales; (2) ridding the store of old merchandise brings in new products;(3) new skills for the associate in training; (4) prepares the store on a day-to-day basis for upcoming sales events.

Accountability   The chosen associate will be responsible for completing the job, including redoing the job until it is complete.

Communication   Explain the job! Explain the selection process! Explain the results and benefits! Explain the accountability! Use written instructions (if available) and spoken communications.

Job   Update layaway file.

Definition   Go through layaway file from *A* to *Z* and update as current, 30 days past due, 60 days past due, and return to stock. Make phone calls or write follow-up letters to all past due people. Return unwanted merchandise to stock—follow up on markdowns.

Selection   Select the associate to complete the job. This may be the associate in training, or pull the layaway information and allow each sales associate to follow up on their own sales.

Results and benefits   (1) Company cash flow; (2) products returned to stock are available for immediate sale; (3) customer contact for additional sales.

Accountability   The chosen associate or associates will be responsible for making the file current and returning all unwanted product back into stock. Perhaps a time limit of 14 days, 21 days, or 30 days should be employed to complete this job.

Communication   Explain the job! Explain the selection! Explain the results and benefits! Explain the accountability! Use written instructions (if available) or spoken communications.

You can use this five-part system on virtually any job/ duty or task you wish to delegate. If you are fortunate enough to already have a detailed policy and/or procedure manual for your operation, this is your source for written communications. If not, you can start to build your own manual to assist with the delegation process. As you complete this five-step system, keep notes, which will be especially helpful for future delegations. Many managers have found great success with using "reader boards" for recurring delegation. As the illustration indicates, rotate your associates from task to task on a weekly basis.

Jobs to Do

Name   *Job*

_____   **BACK ROOM.** Total clean. Sweep and take out the trash.

_____   **DISPLAYS.** Keep all visual looks complete, this includes the windows, cases, counters . . . REPLACE SOLD ITEMS!

_____   **SALES FLOOR.** Vacuum and clean up daily. Dust shelves and counters and sweep.

_____   **BATHROOM.** Clean from top to bottom! Sink, stool, and floor must be spotless.

Many managers have also used a tool like this as a form of motivation. If you have five associates, have only four job slots; the number one sales associate for the week is not included in the system. Some managers keep five job slots for five associates, and then they complete the job duties of their number one sales associate. It is truly amazing just how hard associates will work at being number one when it's their turn to keep the bathroom clean.

Delegate! Don't try to become a supermanager by trying to do everything yourself. Become a supermanager by getting your entire team involved.

SALES MANAGEMENT

To become a great manager, you must learn to love facts, figures, and numbers. However, for many people this is the most difficult part of being a manager. The proper knowledge and application of these elements (or lack of them!) can make or break us.

Sales management requires mastery of three areas:

- Knowledge of the facts and figures (numbers).
- Ability to make comparisons and assessments.
- Development of improvements.

Knowledge of Facts and Figures

Most times you will have easy access to all of the relevant statistics right from the cash registers. They tell us sales per hour, multiple sales percentages, average sale per customer, and total sales. This information should be recorded for the store and each associate. It is best to keep this information on a weekly basis. At the least, record the facts on a monthly basis.

The chart shows the store, six associates, and their numbers for the chosen time period (one week).

Store Average

Sales Per Hour	$	48.00
Multiple Sales		55%
Average Sale	$	33.00
Total Sales	$	1,442.00

BILL:

Sales Per Hour	$	41.00
Multiple Sales		36%
Average Sale	$	27.00
Total Sales	$	1,640.00

SUSAN:

Sales Per Hour	$	46.00
Multiple Sales		84%
Average Sale	$	31.00
Total Sales	$	2,070.00

TIM:

Sales Per Hour	$	31.00
Multiple Sales		12%
Average Sale	$	18.00
Total Sales	$	1,240.00

KAREN:

Sales Per Hour	$	53.00
Multiple Sales		87%
Average Sale	$	51.00
Total Sales	$	1,325.00

JIM:

Sales Per Hour	$	62.00
Multiple Sales		53%
Average Sale	$	29.00
Total Sales	$	1,240.00

DIANE:

Sales Per Hour	$	57.00
Multiple Sales		62%
Average Sale	$	28.00
Total Sales	$	1,140.00

In completing your own performance charts, you may consider separating management from associates, full-time associates from part-time associates, associates employed longer than six months from those less than six months, and so on. The further you break down the charts, the easier it is to compare apples to apples and oranges to oranges.

Make Comparisons and Assessments

Now that you have a chart, you have the ability to compare. Remember to compare apples to apples and oranges to oranges (i.e., it wouldn't be fair to compare your number one person—full time, who has been with you for many months—to the newest part-time person, who has been with you for one week). Using the illustration provided, make an initial assessment. One of the first weaknesses you should notice is Tim's multiple sales percentages—they're very low. In this example you don't know all about Tim, but how would you assess him if the following were true?

- Tim has been with you one week. Perhaps he just needs more training time to develop his skills.
- Tim is always your number one sales associate. Perhaps he had a bad week.
- Tim was involved all week with completely changing the store's layout. Perhaps Tim was preoccupied with his other projects and was trying to do too much.

The shorter the period of time used to complete your charts, the less critical of performance you must be during this time. If, however, you see a pattern developing after several charts, now you have a direction in which to proceed for new improvements. Keep in mind, each associate will have good weeks and bad weeks, good days and bad days, and even good months and bad months.

Several years ago, I witnessed an associate who worked in a men's clothing store. During this time period (1974), the average suit sale was $75. This associate was always in the store average in weekly sales. Then one day, he sold over $9,000 in product; he sold everyone everything he showed them. He had a once-in-a-lifetime day. It would be unfair to expect him to sell $9,000 every day. As well, it's unfair to assume an associate will stay in a selling slump very long.

After a short period of time, associates will develop patterns of performance. From these patterns you will be able to see selling strengths and weaknesses. From there you can use management by exception to help develop improvements.

Develop Improvements

By once again dividing people's strengths and weaknesses, we gain a direction for helping them improve. Using Tim as our example again, we may now have several charts that show his multiple selling percentages are still very low. Perhaps simply working with Tim on selling skills, concentrating on multiple selling, will bring him up to the store average. This is *management by exception*: working with the weaknesses only.

Review the comparison chart for the six associates again. By thinking about delegation, wouldn't this be a perfect job for Susan or Karen, your number one multiple sellers? Most times, just making your associates aware of their shortcomings is enough to spark their efforts at self-improvement. Your job is to give direction.

Often, management has great success after posting this information among the associates. They can see where they stand in relation to the store and others. Use of these charts will be very important as you read the next section, Plan for Success. You will discover just how important they are for your success.

As a side note, the associates' close ratios are one statistic that will not be found by analyzing the cash register information. This ratio is easy to figure and invaluable in your assessments of the associates' strengths and weaknesses. Simply log the number of customers seen by each associate and how many were sold. (Knowledge is a powerful asset. The numbers will surprise everyone.) Do they close 1 out of 10, 2 out of 10, 4 out of 10? If an associate is currently closing 3 out of every 10 customers, and your direction helps him to raise his average to 4 out of every 10 customers, then the associate just posted a 25 percent sales increase. *Know the figures, make comparisons, and develop improvements* with management by exception.

PLAN FOR SUCCESS

Have you ever been plagued by the old adage ''too much— too little—too late''? All too often in business, we rely on others to plan for our success. We're not saying it's wrong for home offices and owners to plan our future sales goals, which often happens months in advance by people thousands of miles away. We're saying it's wrong for you to trust those who engage in the planning while you accept full responsibility for the outcome without knowing if they are correct. We have often listened to managers who say, "It's not my job; the home office (or owner) does this." It *is* your job! How can home offices or owners thousands of miles away, who have made plans months in advance, know your market as well as you do? They can't! We have yet to meet a home office planner or owner who didn't welcome a manager's help and input. The simple fact is, they don't know what you know unless you tell them.

Many critical things rely on a realistic and accurate sales plan: company cash flows, new inventory arrivals, expansion plans, advertising, and hiring new associates, just to name a few. The keys to successful sales planning are *realism* and *accuracy*. All too often we jump into a sales plan without the knowledge or confidence to make the plan. Think about last month. Were you looking for an increase, a decrease, or to remain the same in relation to last year? Did you make last month's sales plan? Did you exceed the plan by more than 5 percent? Did you miss last month's plan by more than 5 percent? When you started last month's plan, did you feel it was just right, too high, or too low?

First of all, you must know your immediate market. What is there for your sales opportunities?

- What is the breakdown of demographics? (Age, sex, occupation, education levels, household incomes, average incomes, employment numbers, area growth, and how many new businesses have recently opened.)
- Who are your customers, and how do they fit into the general demographics? (Age, sex, occupation, educa-

tion levels, household incomes, average incomes, and
employment numbers.)

* What has changed in your market over the past
month, six months, one year? (New jobs, layoffs,
market growth, market decline.)

Look at the following example and see how the market
changes by lowering the unemployment rate by just 1
percent. If your marketing area has a base population of
200,000 and the unemployment rate drops by 1 percent,
this means 2,000 more people have jobs. If their average
income (take-home) is $1,600 per month, their combined
incomes add an additional $3.2 million per month into
the marketplace, or an additional $38.4 million annually.
If the customer base commits 5 percent of their income
to your business category for purchases of products or
services, this equals $1,920,000. If your business enjoys
a 7 percent market share ownership, this provides the
opportunity to add $134,400 to your cash register. All
from the lowering of unemployment by 1 percent. If your
store does $1 million per year in volume, adding $134,400
is a 13.4 percent sales increase. Remember, the numbers
work both ways.

Do your home offices, owners, regional managers, or
district managers know these facts? They don't know unless you tell them.

Amazingly, all of the facts and information are readily
available. Your local chamber of commerce office has information. If your store is located in a controlled shopping
center, the management team has a marketing plan. Get
the information!

Second, know your sales associates and their abilities—
skills, sales per hour, average sale, multiple selling, total
sales, and how they compare to last year's staff. To assist
your investigation, you may find it easier to use a planning
sheet like the one illustrated.

Store Plan for the Month of: _____

I. Prior Year Total Sales .... _____
   Sales Per Hour .... _____
   Multiple Percentages .... _____
   Average Sale .... _____

II. Prior Year Store and/or Mall Promotions: _____

III. Prior Year Market Conditions: _____

IV. Current Sales Plan .... _____
    Amount of Increase (Decrease) .... _____
    Sales Per Hour Needed .... _____
    Multiple Percentages Needed .... _____
    Average Sale Needed .... _____

Are the current associates capable of the sales plan?

V. Current Store and/or Mall Promotions: _____

VI. Current Market Conditions: _____

Notes:

Many managers have found it beneficial to place things on paper; it's easier to work with. After you have completed a quick assessment of the situation, you are in a position (have the knowledge) to agree or disagree with the upcoming plan. You will see three possible assumptions:

1. The sales plan is just right. It can be met, but it's still going to be a challenge. Pat yourself on the back for doing a good job of investigation, and move forward into the sales plan.

2. The sales plan is too high. Be careful. When you make this determination, the plan *is* too high. Redo your investigation just to make sure you didn't miss any details. As simplistic as this may seem, the only alternative to an overly ambitious sales plan is to lower it. Although difficult, it is better to adjust your expectations before the fact rather than scramble around in a panic. When you confront the higher-

ups, be prepared to present the appropriate facts and figures to support your theory. A goal that is too high only
frustrates everyone involved—the home office or owner is
upset because the plan wasn't met, and the sales staff may
feel substandard because the plan wasn't met.

Be careful. As you are now armed with all of this new
knowledge, your first reaction will be to call the home office
and the owner and tell them of your wonderful information. At first you will feel like you have wasted your time—
no one will listen. Continue to provide knowledge and information. The home office or owner may or may not adjust
the sales plan; either way, stay involved.

A sales plan that is too high can cause some problems.
As everything is relative to sales activity, consider the following:

- The store may now be overstocked on inventory and
  you may have to wait for future shipments—the new
  spring, fall, summer, or winter lines; new products;
  or store exclusives.

- The store may have spent too much money on advertising in relation to sales activity. If you overspend the
  budget by 1.5 percent this month, you must underspend by this amount at some point in the future,
  thus making future sales harder to achieve.

- You scheduled your associates for too many hours in
  relation to sales activity. The sales floor is too crowded.
  Friendly associate competition now turns into unfriendly activity. You cut back hours and you, the
  manager, need to make them up, thus causing you a
  heavier workload, which cuts into your effectiveness.

3. The sales plan is too low. Simply put, it's too easy and
presents no challenge. If, after all of your investigation, you
believe the sales plan is too low, have it raised! Having a
sales plan that is too low for your abilities is far more damaging than having one that is too high. See what happens:

- Instead of having too much inventory, there isn't enough. The store could start to lose its sales momentum. The spring, fall, summer, or winter lines could have arrived earlier, or the store could have received exclusives sooner than the competition did, not later or at the same time.

- Instead of spending too much on advertising, we spend too little. (No doubt a group of accountants is saying, "This is great, we could underspend and save.") But additional advertising dollars could have been used to attract more customers, which could have been developed into repeat customers.

- Instead of scheduling too many hours, we didn't schedule enough. Now you won't have adequate coverage on the sales floor, thus opening your store to a serious customer service problem. Customers feel ignored, and the sales associates are hurried and perhaps don't make the volume of sales they would have made with proper sales assistance.

Let's pretend we're yo-yos. The store is given a 5 to 7 percent sales increase (goal) for the month. But the store does a 28 percent increase. The home office or owner notices your sterling performance and ups the next month's goal by 25 percent. But, at about the time you made last month's easy plan, you began to relax (it's human nature to relax when the project is complete) and slow down on your aggression. You have now lost momentum, and you increase sales by just 2 to 3 percent the next month (and you worked your rear end off just getting that). The home office or owner notices and responds by lowering the next month's plan back to 5 to 7 percent increases. But now you have regained your momentum, and your sales increase is once again above 25 percent. Isn't this game fun?

To summarize, investigate everything, and contribute information to others when they make sales plans for you.

Be willing to change things if necessary. Utilize all of your resources to ensure the development of a realistic and accurate plan. Make a commitment and then single-mindedly lead the team to pursue the goal. Your career, performance reviews, salary increases, and promotions all depend on the consistent achievement of your monthly sales plans.

Every manager today has the opportunity to be part of an elite group—managers who make things happen. The magic word is *opportunity*. It's all up to you. Don't expect overnight success as a manager or assume your associates will give you instant respect just because you are the manager. Success and respect must be earned.

Chapter Five

Management Self-Evaluation

INTRODUCTION

P ersonal development—it's the rage! What started out as a trend in the mid-1960s has escalated into a lifestyle. Popular are:

- Self-help books, tapes, and videos on virtually any subject matter.
- Attending college and returning to school.
- Attending seminars.
- Joining self-help groups.
- Joining health clubs.
- Reductions in smoking and alcohol consumption, and increased drug awareness.
- Cosmetic surgery.

With the wealth of information and activities available in the personal development industry, our society has become perfect—we always work for the good; we are all well educated; we all have perfect bodies; we all eat healthy foods;

we have stopped smoking; we have all said no to drugs. Basically, we're perfect—or are we? As you examine the reasons why some can advance their personal development while others can't seem to achieve this goal, you will see that the real answer lies with our ability to adapt to change.

"Change is not a sign of weakness. There is nothing wrong with change, if it is in the right direction. To improve is to change, so to be perfect is to have changed often."

— Winston Churchill

The goal of the next sections in this book is not to provide all of the answers. In reality, this would be virtually impossible. Rather, the information concentrates on specific areas that will help you in your day-to-day store environment.

MANAGEMENT BY EXCEPTION

"It is because of your strengths that you have achieved your current level of success. But it is because of your weaknesses that you haven't achieved a higher level."

Know yourself! And be honest! *Management by exception* is the management of your strengths and weaknesses. To make any change or improvement, the weaknesses must be transformed into strengths. It is essential to continue to build your strengths; but for change and improvement, it is critical to concentrate more time and energy on your weak areas.

In the retail world, we wear many hats—salesperson, inventory controller, motivator, bookkeeper, trainer, problem solver, customer service specialist, and many others. Because we are called on to perform and accept many different challenges, it's critical to use the management by exception methods.

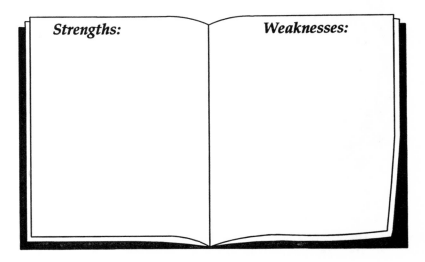

| *Strengths:* | *Weaknesses:* |

Most often, a *strength* is something you are good at and enjoy doing. On the other hand, a *weakness* is something you don't enjoy and are not especially good at performing.

First, begin to analyze and understand. Make two lists. On the first, begin to list all of your strengths. On the second, begin to list all of your weaknesses. Don't try to make your lists all at once. Take up to 30 days or longer to complete the lists. It is crucial to be honest with yourself. As you evaluate yourself, take into account everything that takes place. For example, the general term *selling* may be listed as a strength, but overcoming objections may be a weakness. You may feel you are positive, but not when confronted with customer complaints. In essence, be as detailed as possible with your lists. And if you are having trouble making a list, recruit your associates to help you. Believe me! They will know your strengths and weaknesses better than anyone.

After your lists are completed, work with one weakness at a time until you feel it has become a strength. Then move on to another and another and another. Some weaknesses may take only a few hours of concentration and action, while others may require days, weeks, months, or years of concentrated effort. Keep in mind, you may never change certain weaknesses into strengths. But you know yourself and your limitations. Continue to update, change, and revise your lists. Doing this exercise is not a once-in-a-lifetime feat—it's ongoing.

Knowing yourself will help you direct your energies and activities. After many days, weeks, months, or years of trying to turn a weakness into a strength, if you feel it's not going to happen, accept the fact. But you now know it's a lingering weakness, and the challenge should be given to someone who recognizes this as a strength.

Next, have your associates complete this same exercise of knowing their strengths and weaknesses. Once this information is known, you as the manager have precise direction to build everyone as a team as based on their strengths. And, you have knowledge to help turn their weaknesses into more strengths.

Management by exception was developed for two reasons: (1) as a directional tool for delegating and incorporating a team concept and (2) for time management. In today's retail environment, you don't have time to do more than analyze the general concept, find the weakness, and fix it. Most of all, be honest with yourself.

STRESS MANAGEMENT

Stress is defined as a nonspecific response to any demand or change on your body or brain. The response is nonspecific because stress affects everyone differently. Everyone may react differently to stress. The changes or demands placed on us can be good or bad; however, they all cause some degree of stress. A promotion could be perceived as good—more money, more responsibility, a move up. But it's guaranteed to cause more stress, because it is a change. People are often asked why they don't like to change. The main reason lies here: it causes stress.

GAS

Within our physical makeup, we have a biological mechanism that allows us to adapt to stress and accommodate it. This mechanism is called the general adaptation syndrome, or GAS. GAS either leads to control or allows us to exhaust ourselves. The important factor is to know your limitations. GAS has three stages.

1. Alarm   This is also called the flight-or-fight response. The alarm stage is a built-in internal survival mechanism that allows us to react as we have been trained to do or as we have done in the past through experiences. Most times we don't even think, we just react. If you have ever had to swerve your car to avoid a collision, you have felt the alarm stage of stress. The stress symptoms produced in the alarm stage include sweaty palms, tense muscles, increased heart rate, or rapid breathing. Usually this response is an overreaction that hurts more than it helps. Fortunately, most retailers don't spend much of their time in the alarm stage. The constant reminder of this type of stress will quickly cause overloads.

In contrast, police officers spend much of their lives within the alarm stage, and they are trained to react to it. Imagine spending 20 or 30 years of your life not knowing what is around the next corner. Then take away the constant stress. We're told by law enforcement experts that the loss of stress is even more damaging than the stress. Stress is like a double-edged sword.

2. Resistance This is where most of our lives are spent. The resistance stage is where our bodies and minds try to adapt and control the stress. If you have a method to deal with the stress, then negative stress is avoided. If not, then you will find yourself in the third stage.

3. Exhaustion (Better known as wacked-out, two bricks shy of a load, off in left field, ready for the bug house, or many other sayings.) In this final stage, stress runs rampant, far outweighing your ability to adapt to its increased demands. The exhaustion stage makes you susceptible to a variety of physical and mental ailments. These leave you with a run-down, unsure-of-yourself feeling.

Examine some of the symptoms of stress—the physical or mental ailments you may feel during the resistance and exhaustion stages of stress.

Symptoms of STRESS

Expression of boredom.

Problems making decisions.

Loss of concentration.

Not knowing whom to trust.

Feelings of persecution.

Sudden weight loss or gain.

Change in smoking habits.

Change in use of alcohol.

Change in social hours.

Difficulty being with others.

Sudden change in appearance.

Persistent physical problems.

Bodily pain (eyes, neck, shoulders, head).

Procrastination.

Forgetfulness.

Loss of appetite.

Loss of energy.

Lack of organization.

Difficulty sleeping.

Poor posture.

Accident prone.

Frequent headaches.

Sudden allergies.

Feeling of confusion.

Afternoon run-down.

Increase in colds or infections.

This list is by no means complete. These are but a few of the dozens and dozens of stress symptoms. There isn't a magic number of symptoms to indicate you're in the resistance stage or the exhaustion stage. If you exhibit 20 of these symptoms from the current stress in your life and you don't feel exhausted, then it's OK. But if you are exhibiting five and feel you are out of control, then it's too much. In essence, you must know yourself! Only you can decide how much stress is too much and how much is tolerable. But one thing is very clear: you can condition yourself to accept more stress. For example, a promotion to store manager in another state is a change, a stress. It may involve many changes, such as leaving family and friends, finding a place to live, dealing with higher costs of living, contacting the phone company and the gas company for new hook-ups, working in a low-volume store, and meeting new sales staff. Within 30 to 60 days, most of the changes have been completed—they are not sources of stress anymore. Now, transfer to a new store and repeat this process. In most instances, the next move would be easier because you have done it before. The next move is easier, and the next move is even easier, and so on. This is not to say the move is any more pleasant, it's just easier to do. Why? Because in your experiences, you have gained knowledge to make each move less stressful. This same experience will allow you to adjust to most of the changes you will face day in and day out in your retail environment.

Causes of Stress

What causes stress? In reality, only two factors cause stress—external events and internal events. Let's look at both.

1. External *External stress* is defined as a change over which you have little or no control. External stresses are caused by someone or something else. These may be:

- A car pulling out in front of you.
- Being stuck in traffic.
- Waiting in line.
- Time deadlines.
- Taxes.
- An associate who calls in sick.
- Merchandise not arriving.
- The cash register breaks down.
- A visit from the district manager.

The stress experts tell us only about 10 percent of the stress in our lives is external.

2. Internal   Are we our own worst enemies? The answer is a very loud *yes! Internal stress* is caused by our perception of our business lives, our personal lives, and ourselves. This type of stress is created in our minds and may include:

- Overreactions to situations, people, places, or events.
- Unfulfilled expectations of people and relationships.
- Unrealistically high plans and goals.
- Worries about uncertainties and uncontrollable events.
- Preoccupation with worst-case situations.

Are we our own worst enemies? Yes, we are! As well, keep in mind that any internal stress is influenced by its intensity, duration, and the added effect of other stress causers.

Combatting Stress

Following are a wide variety of methods you can use to combat stress. The following methods are identified as from the medical experts.

Diet As you were growing up, your health teachers at school told you about the importance of a balanced diet. Of course, in the retail industry, this is easier said than done. Often we are reduced to eating junk foods, cold pizza, and warm soda. It has often been said, ''If times are slow, get some lunch or dinner and it's sure to bring in customers.''

Junk foods and refined sugars are high in calories and fat and low in food value. Food is your fuel, so make it high-octane. Eating well and limiting your use of salt, sugar, caffeine, and alcohol can promote health and help reduce stress. If possible, take a vitamin supplement high in vitamin B to help overcome fatigue. If at all possible, try to establish regular meal times and stick to them. Get out of the store—a change in environment will help.

General perception A key to stress control is to change your perception of events and people. If you are your own worst enemy, recognize it! Lower your expectations of people—including yourself! It is always better to expect less and receive more than to expect more and receive less. Be aware of your negative self-thoughts. If you tend to worry, go ahead and worry! Then forget about it. When you examine your worrisome attitude, you will most likely find all of the worrying you did would not have changed the outcome. With practice and self-control, you will be able to combat negative self-thought and your overaggressive perceptions.

Guided imagination In a darkened room, take a quick vacation. You can do this with or without gentle background music. Now, close your eyes and create theater of the mind by viewing a relaxing scene. Picture yourself being the first person to ride up the ski lift, noticing the trees, the birds, the fresh snowfall from the previous night. Exit the lift, and now you are the first person down the perfect slope. Look at your ski tips as they float through six inches of fresh powder. The only sound you hear is the ski against the fresh snow. Or take a walk on a secluded beach, or scuba dive, or hang glide, or work in a garden, or bike ride on a secluded mountain pass. Relax and go where your imagination takes you.

Exercise Physically fit people handle stress more easily than those who are out of shape. And fit folks tend to feel better about themselves in general. Bike ride, work out at the gym, run, walk, lift weights, ski, play basketball—do whatever makes you feel good. Before you start an intense, full-blown exercise program, visit your doctor and get a physical exam. It may sound stupid to tell your doctor, ''I'm thinking of bending at the waist. What do you think?'' But the doctor will help you with an exercise routine that is right for your age and general physical condition. A routine exercise schedule's magic is that once you start, you will actually look forward to the relaxation that exercise can bring.

Relaxation The following will detail two quick relaxation exercises that can be performed right at the store.

Progressive relaxation is done in a sitting or reclining position, perhaps at the desk in the back room. In this technique, all you do is tense specific muscles, hold them for five seconds, and release them. Don't hold your breath, but continue to breathe deeply as you focus on the muscle groups. Start with your feet, then move to your calves, buttocks, fingers, arms, shoulders, neck, and chin. Repeat this process in reverse order until you feel better. Many people say they feel better and more relaxed in about five minutes. The magic of progressive relaxation is it can be done while you are doing other store business.

Break time relaxation is a perfect time to pamper yourself. Try to set a specific time each day (break time) to complete these steps, once in the morning and once in the afternoon. Start with a forehead and sinus area massage. Gently rub between and under your eyes. With open hands, rub around the eye sockets without pressing on the eye. All movements should start at the center, working up and out. Next, work your eyes. Start with your eyes looking straight ahead. Now, look to the left as far as you can, then back to the center. Look to the right as far as you can, then back to the center. Repeat this two more times.

Continue on by looking up as far as you can—keep your head still—then back to the center. Now look down as far as you can, then back to the center. Repeat this two more times. Remember, move only your eyes.

The neck area is next. Move your head forward and then back. Start with short movements and then work up to touching your chin to your chest and your head back as far as it will go. Then move on to side-to-side movements by placing your chin on each shoulder. Then try to touch your ears to your shoulders. Finish with neck rolls by moving your head counterclockwise and then clockwise.

The last area is the shoulders. Start with your shoulders relaxed. Rotate your shoulders to the front by creating circles, then reverse the rotation. Start with small circles and gradually work up to large circles.

As you have noticed, the break time exercises have concentrated on the eyes, neck, and shoulders. These are the areas most people talk about when they feel stressed. The last two areas of combatting stress will complete the picture.

Self-help   There is no greater method of combatting stress than to take the bull by the horns and deal with it. Follow the formula and take action!

- List the stresses you are facing.
- Identify the most common symptoms.
- List how you cope with the stress.
- Rate how you cope—positive or negative.
- Change negatives to positives.

Apply the formula in this way:

Stress—meeting monthly sales plan.

Identify—feeling pressure, nervous, can't sleep, headaches.

Cope—take aspirin, drink lots of coffee, work 70 hours a week, and worry all the time.

Rate—negative: drinking too much coffee, working too many hours, and having negative self-thought.

Change—drink decaffeinated coffee, delegate more work, be aware of the negative self-thought, and work on an exercise program.

Get therapy   This is not therapy at the doctor's office. This is therapy you create yourself. Find an activity or a hobby in which you can become totally engrossed. The activity or hobby should require your complete concentration to be good at it. By focusing your complete attention on the activity, your mind must leave all of its other worries behind. Activities like gardening, mowing, painting, arts and crafts, metalworking, sailing, flying, and even parachuting are great therapy. Sports are even better. They require your concentration and give you exercise at the same time. Golf, tennis, skiing, swimming, racketball, and organized sports like basketball, softball, and volleyball leagues are perfect therapies.

When stress is good   At first this may sound like a crazy statement. After all, the previous pages have been devoted to recognizing stress and combatting it. Within your mental makeup, you are attracted to the risks and challenges associated with doing a good job—in fact, of being number one for your company. Most people perform at their best when some level of stress is associated with their job. If you are not challenged with making the monthly sales goal, why bother? If you are not challenged by taking over a subperforming operation, why bother? If there is no risk associated in motivating your associates, why bother?

Stress can be good! We will perform at our best when faced with a challenge or a risk. Your objective is to know how much is enough and how much is too much.

Stress is a fact of life, but it needn't be a way of life! Remember, we can't control many things in our personal and business lives (external stresses), but most stress is controllable. Your experiences will still be one of your best teachers. Remember your first driving lesson—hands at 10 and 2, watch your speed, look for traffic signs, use your turn signal, and a million other concerns. After a short period of time, driving a car became second nature. In truth, the more you perform jobs, tasks, duties/responsibilities— live life—you will be able to stop stress simply by experience and becoming accustomed to the event.

TIME MANAGEMENT

Know your worth! If you begin to think about time and its concepts, you will realize just how valuable it is. When you realize that time has a value (just like money), it becomes important to spend your time like a careful consumer. When you take a closer look at time, the fat can be trimmed from your schedule. Once this is done, you will have more time left for the things that are truly important and valuable to your operation.

Know your time worth. Please don't confuse this with your monthly salary or hourly wages. For your *time worth*, add the following:

100% of your salary (monthly)	$_____
40% of your salary for fringe benefits	_____
100% of your subordinate associates' salaries	_____
40% of their salaries for fringe benefits	_____
Total	$_____

Next, divide the total by the number of hours you spend on key management responsibilities. (Typical managers will spend one-third of their total time on true management duties.)

Total hours worked	_____
¹⁄₃ of total hours	_____
Worth per hour	$_____

An example may look as follows (monthly):

100% of your salary	$2,000
40% for fringe benefits	800
100% of subordinates' salaries	8,587
40% of their salaries for fringes	3,435
Total	$14,822
Total hours worked (55 per week)	220
¹⁄₃ of total hours	73
Worth per hour	$203

If the above example were true for your situation, ask yourself if it is worth its price tag. Should someone worth $203 per hour

Clean the bathroom?

Check in inventory?

Take out the trash?

Sell?

Work with customer problems?

Train and develop associates?

Recruit new associates?

Motivate?

Is it worth your time? As stated, please con't confuse this worth with your salary; chances are they're far apart. But this exercise will show you what time is worth to you.

When doing this time worth exercise, you will once again

see one very important word: *delegating!* If a duty, project, or job is not worth your time but still must be done, delegate it to another associate.

Time Wasters

Following is a list of common time wasters. Read the statements and choose your top five time wasters. Place a 1 beside the statement that best describes your biggest time waster. Continue in descending order until you have selected your top five time wasters. *Read the entire list before you mark on it.* If your time wasters are not listed, please list them.

_____ A lot of time is wasted because the associates lack direction.

_____ I spend a lot of time going from store emergency to store emergency. I waste time being a crisis manager.

_____ I waste time trying to please more than one boss.

_____ I spend too much time with paperwork and red tape.

_____ I spend too much time answering questions for the associates.

_____ The equipment—cash register, calculator, and so on—never works right.

_____ I waste time because I'm not motivated.

_____ The telephone constantly interrupts my day.

_____ The daily flow of visitors, friends, salespeople and so on disrupts my day.

_____ I have too many irons in the fire. My inability to say no makes me spend too much time on other projects.

_____ I waste time by not completing a project before I take on new ones.

_____ I pay too much attention to the minor problems.

_____ I waste time when I don't receive clear and complete instructions.

_____

_____

Know Yourself

To begin being an effective time manager, you must first know yourself. In the following characteristics, there are no rights or wrongs. The important thing is to know yourself.

Morning or night person   Morning people wake up early, refreshed and ready to go! Their most productive hours are before noon, and they are usually worn out by late afternoon or early evening. Night people, on the other hand, like to stay up late. These people wake up slowly, and they are hitting their peak hours in early afternoon. Try to schedule your most difficult tasks during your peak hours of performance.

Intensive or extensive worker   Intensive workers find it easy to concentrate for highly productive short spurts of time. They burn out easily and find it difficult to sit down and complete a project from start to finish without a break or two. Extensive workers will be just as productive, but they can sit and work until a project is finished in one sitting. For example, an intensive worker may take three one-hour time periods during three days to complete a project, while an extensive worker may take one three-hour time period.

Type A or Type B personality   Type A workers are compulsive workers. They have to be doing something all of the time—work, work, work. They seem nervous and don't like to sit down. They like sports and group activities. Type B people are quieter than their compulsive counterparts. They won't proceed with a project until it is well thought out. In most instances, a Type B personality is well organized and attuned to detail. Keep in mind, both types will get the job done, they just do it differently. A Type A and Type B comparison is like watching two different comedians at work. Howie Mandel, who jumps around the stage, is a Type A person; Steven Wright, who never cracks a smile, is portrayed as a Type B person. They both get the job done—they make you laugh. They just do it differently.

Duty oriented or people oriented   Duty-oriented people like to take on long-term projects that can keep them isolated for long periods of time. Engineers, accountants, architects, and the so-called paperwork people fit into this category. People-oriented people thrive on dealing with colleagues and associates. They must have interaction with people. Salespeople are the leaders in this category. As managers, we must wear both hats. If we dislike paperwork projects, try to schedule them during our peak hours of effectiveness.

The key is to know and understand yourself and know that your personalities can change as do your job requirements. We live in cycles. When we were small children, we could get up early. In fact, 5:30 or 6 AM was "sleeping in." When we became teenagers, we were lucky to be out of bed before noon, but we could stay up way past 1 or 2 in the morning. Now, as we become older, we find it easier to get up early once again. The same will hold true as your management life changes. Today, imagine yourself as a store manager with seven associates. Your personalities may be morning person, intensive worker, Type A, and a people-oriented manager. Then, promote yourself to a district manager position. You may then find yourself being an evening person (mornings are for travel), extensive worker, Type B, and duty oriented to manage your time better. Remain flexible and open to change.

Steps of Time Management

Once you have a full understanding of the four basic characteristics—know the whos, whats, whens, wheres, and whys—you can now set up an effective time management outline.

Lists   Divide your lists into three categories:

- Top priorities.
- Low priorities.
- Long-term projects.

Clarify the priorities   Your number one concern as a manager is sales and anything to do with sales. Each time you have a specific project to complete, ask yourself this question: If I don't do this, will I reach my objective (sales plan)? If the answer is yes, then it's a low priority. If, however, the answer is no, then it's a top priority. Categorize your projects on this one objective—sales. Examples may include:

- Sales meeting—top priority.
- New inventory on the sales floor—top priority.
- Straighten back room—low priority.
- Train new associate on store closing procedures—low priority.
- Develop a new recruiting strategy—long-term project with top priority.

Plan your time   Purchase and use a planner to help with your daily, weekly, and monthly schedules. If you don't purchase a planner, make your own—it will help with organizational skills.

First, fill in all of the normal, routine projects, duties, and appointments that take up your time on a weekly or monthly basis. These may include:

- Preparing weekly schedules.
- Compiling sales figures and reports.
- Maintenance schedules.
- Store meetings.

- Training schedules.
- Performance reviews.
- Outside salespeople visits—advertisers, suppliers, and so on.

Remember your objective   Focus on sales when you are filling in your time schedules. A word of warning: at first, after instituting a priority-based work schedule, you will feel like super time manager. Don't worry, this feeling will soon go away. You may have scheduled the hours of 10:30 AM to noon on Monday to complete your store reports. But after seven phone calls, one customer problem, 17 customers, a shipment received, and two unscheduled advertising salespeople, it's now 3 PM and you haven't even had lunch yet, let alone looked at the reports. Stay flexible and remain patient.

Get others involved!   This is the savior of your time management schedules. Once you have filled in your weekly and/or monthly planner, make a list of top priorities, low priorities, and long-term projects to delegate to your other associates. Let them get involved. *You can't do it all by yourself!*

Procrastination   Everyone has been guilty of this at one time or another. A little bit won't hurt your overall performance. But the problem starts when you put some things off and off and off until it becomes a crisis, which requires you to rush into the project and, most times, rush through it. Each time we delay the inevitable, the task becomes less appealing and desirable. Many times you must complete a project but just don't want to! You must convince yourself that the end result of the dreaded job is well worth the time and trouble. As a side note, when you find yourself procrastinating, it's most likely a job you don't like. There are also some direct correlations between stress symptoms and procrastination. If you find yourself procrastinating more than usual, you could be at the breaking point in your ability to cope with stress.

In conclusion, time management requires you to:

- Focus on your objective—sales, not activities.
- Record a time log periodically to analyze how you use your time.
- Be determined to rid yourself of bad habits.
- Eliminate at least one time waster each week.
- Make a to-do list every day and include your associates.
- Make sure your first hour of peak time is the most productive.
- Take time to do it right the first time.
- Develop a habit of finishing what you start.
- Learn to do it now.
- Get others involved by delegating.

"Give me a store clerk with a goal, and I will show you a man who will make history. Give me a man without a goal, and I will show you a store clerk."

— JC Penney
Founder
JC Penney Company

GOALS

Are you a day dreamer or a goal setter? The only real difference is that daydreams are thoughts we keep to ourselves while goals are written, assessed, changed, and accomplished in a logical sequence of events. Everyone daydreams. We dream about wealth, success, winning the lottery, the new car, the promotion, and many other prizes. Daydreaming is healthy! It's like taking a quick vacation in your mind. Goals are even more healthy. In many instances, a goal turns our dreams into reality. The experts tell us that only 3 to 4 percent of all people make goals. (Isn't it amazing how this percentage matches the percentages of the elite group of managers who make things happen?) People don't make goals because of one or more of four reasons:

- They don't know how.
- They are afraid they won't reach their goals and will feel embarrassed or let down.
- They don't know why they should make goals.
- They have a poor self-image and feel they really don't deserve the good things in life.

Goal setting is not new. J C Penney made his statement about goals back in the early 1900s, yet it still rings true today!

How to Set Goals

Goals have certain elements, parts, and characteristics that make them real.

1. The goal must be big, tough, and a challenge. It will take such a big, tough goal to create the excitement necessary for its accomplishment. There isn't any excitement in something average. However, this is all

relative. What may be big and tough for me may not be for you, and vice versa. Be careful about letting others make goals for you. The goal-setting process is an individual activity. At the least, be a part of the goal setting.

2. The goal must be long term. It's OK to have short-term goals, things that must be accomplished this day, this week, or in one month. But, these short-term accomplishments are only part of the big picture. A long-term goal may be to make the year's sales plan. The short-term goals are the monthly, weekly, or daily goals that make up the big picture. If your goals are not long term, you will tend to view any minor shortcomings as goal stoppers. Focus on the long-range picture!

3. The goal must be planned. The entire process of planning the goal will be much easier if you put things to paper and utilize the following parts.

Goal: Date:

What is needed to accomplish this goal:

What obstacles are in the way:

Expected benefit of reaching the goal:

Date to finish the goal:

Signature: Witness:
_____   _____

These parts allow you to think, use logic, investigate, and determine whether the goal is obtainable and realistic.

The goal Be specific: try to reduce the goal to numbers if possible, such as a $30,000 increase in sales, or 10 percent higher multiple percentages, or increase the average sale by $2, or save $75 from each paycheck for the down payment on the new car. When we reduce goals to numbers or some quantified item, they are easier to plan. If the goal can't be reduced to numbers, state ideal conditions for meeting the goal. For example, if the goal is to organize the office, state the ideal end result.

The date This is your starting date. For the goal to be accomplished, it must first be started.

What obstacles are in the way These are the stepping stones, not the stopping stones. The obstacles are things that will try to prevent you from reaching your goal. They may be inventory problems, shipping dates, braces for the kids, car repairs, losing your number one salesperson to transfer, and so on. Don't try to overcome your obstacles—problems and concerns—before you start the goal. If you do, you most likely will never get started. Just be aware of things that can go wrong and don't be surprised (remember crisis management).

Expected benefit of reaching the goal This is your prize, perk, present, or gift. It's highly unlikely you will ever put your best foot forward into reaching the goal if there isn't some type of reward at the end. This may be a raise, of being number one in the region, division, or company, or the vacation of a lifetime, or your new house, or the new car, or many other benefits. Tell yourself what it is you will get for reaching the goal.

Date to finish the goal This is your deadline! The goal has a start date, and it must have a completion date. The goal can not go on and on and on. It must stop somewhere so you can gauge the final event—success or failure.

Signature and witness   Your signature will be your commitment to reaching the stated goal. This is like buying something on credit. When you sign the loan papers, your reputation is on the line to make the payments. The banker who signed as a witness to your promise to make good on the loan says, in essence, "I believe you." But most important, the witness is there to help! You will be amazed when you enlist others to help you reach your goal. They will remind you of the goal and offer help and encouragement; they want you to make it! If you don't believe this, promise something to someone special in your life—wife, husband, boyfriend, girlfriend, or child. Then, watch how much they will help you keep your promise. They will remind you each and every day about the vacation to Hawaii, the new diamond ring, the new car, the special trip to Disneyland, or whatever you promised them. The same will hold true with your business goals. A district manager, a regional manager, an owner, or a store associate will help you reach the goals. If the goal is storewide, everyone signs the goal sheet.

Get started!   The final element of a goal-planning sheet and the goal process is to get started! How many times have you had a great idea, a thought, a daydream, but it never became a reality because the first step was never taken? We all have had, or still have, closets and drawers full of ideas and daydreams, but they will never do any good if we don't get started.

The illustration shows a practical application of the goal-planning sheet and how yours may look. The goal sheet can be used for any business or personal goal; just follow the format. Many managers have found success by placing

Goal: Increase the store's multiple sales percentage by 15%.

Date: May 1, 199—

What Is Needed to Accomplish the Goal: Special sales meetings and training. Constant communication and reinforcement. 1½ more customers buying out of every 10.

	Store at 55%	Review:	Now	New
	Need 70%	Bill	36	56
		Susan	84	84
No increase required, but any will help make up shortage of others		Jim	12	48
		Jon	53	68
		Karen	87	87
		Diane	62	74

What Obstacles Are in the Way:

* Someone not participating
* Loss of Susan or Karen to transfer?
* Expect a drop at first — everyone trying to hard?

Expected Benefit of Reaching the Goal:

#1 in the region. Sales increases!
Average customer sale increased, possible raises!
Pizza party on me each month we hit 15% plus!

Date to Finish:

May 1, 199— (one year)

Signature:

Jon Smith

Witness: Susen Thompson
Jim Jones
Bill Brown
Karen Jackson
Dan Miller

them on walls in the back room, or the store's announcements area—the bulletin board.

Years ago when I started the company, I had a goal of turning my skills, knowledge, and expertise into a book that would benefit others. Ten years later (long term), the goal is now finished. But the goal had a start date; I knew what was needed to accomplish it, what obstacles were in the way, and its benefits; it had a finish date; and I had witnesses. Over the 10 years it took to bring my goal to reality, it was a constant textbook example of successes and failures, tests and trials and error. In the end, I stuck with it and turned my daydream into reality. You can do the same with your daydreams and goals.

Now that we are past the first reason why people don't make goals, let's examine the other three.

Embarrassed or Let Down?

You bet! The next time you are gathered with a group of friends and peers, stand up and state that you have an announcement to make. Tell everyone in the group something that may seem impossible on the surface. An example may be, Next year at this time, I will be driving a brand new Mercedes Benz 560SLC, or I will be number one in the company, or I'm going to post a 50 percent increase in sales. The first reaction from your peers may be Yeah, right. What bank are you going to rob? You are ranked 47th in the company now, and you will be number 1 next year—good luck. But the fact is, they will expect you to hold good on what you told them. If you are not driving the new Mercedes, or if you are not number one in the company, or if you haven't increased sales by 50 percent, your friends and peers will be right there to tease, taunt, and embarrass you for not obtaining what you told them you would.

Realism and accuracy are critical in making goals work. If you plan things on paper and you realistically feel you can be number one in the company—jumping from 47th to 1st—then go for it! If, however, after all of your planning, you can jump from 47th to 25th in one year, this should be your goal. Then from 25th to 15th, from 15th to 8th, from 8th to 3rd, and finally from 3rd to 1st.

A recurring problem is our tendency to overrate our expectations of ourselves. Remember, we can be our own worst enemy. The point is, don't set yourself up for failure. Be realistic and accurate with the goal-setting process. And finally, so what if you don't reach every goal? You have nothing to feel embarrassed about. Chances are the person who would tease or taunt you has never had the guts to even try.

Why Make Goals?

In essence, goals give our lives direction and purpose. Without goals, we will never know if we have achieved what we set out to accomplish. The decision to make goals or to not make goals is totally yours. But if you decide to not make goals, imagine the following and the problems associated with it.

You need to go to Paris, Texas. You can't ask anyone how to get there, you have no idea if you reach this location by driving, flying, boat, or train. You can't use a road map, and you are not allowed to read the road signs. In essence, you're on your own to make it there. Would you have any problems making this trip. You can count on it! It's highly unlikely you would ever arrive at your destination.

The same theory holds true for anything you want to do. Make a goal, long term, plan it out—realistic and accurate—and get started. And, yes, there is a place called Paris, Texas. You could go there if you had the right tools, directions, proper transportation, maps, and the use of road signs. Take the opportunity to give yourself as much direction and purpose as possible.

A Poor Self-Image

As surprising as this may sound, it's more true in many cases than you may think. Every day you are bombarded by images that remind you of your subpar existence. These images include:

- Driving the right automobile.
- Finishing your master's degree.
- Having your hair cut at the right hair salon.
- Losing weight at the right weight control center.
- Joining the right health club.
- Looking like the models on television—aren't they all perfect?
- Eating at the right restaurant.

This list could go on and on and on.

In essence, after viewing ourselves in this subpar existence, we feel stupid, uninformed, out of style, overweight, and ugly, eat the wrong foods, and drive the wrong car. The psychiatric community agrees that it doesn't take long for people to start to believe what others tell them. Then, once a person develops a low self-image, it's very hard to come back out of it.

It's often said that the advertising community could use a dose of reality. A perfect example is the health club/home workout industry. Most health clubs and home workout videos show the perfect person. Rippling muscles, Mel Gibson or Cindy Crawford drop-dead good looks, great hair, never sweating are all part of the picture. However, one of the most successful people in this industry is Richard Simmons. His programs show real people, with messy hair, sometimes overweight, and sweating! He shows reality.

Then, to further compound the problems of low self-image, we live in an instant society—instant everything and instant gratification. This includes instant breakfast, instant style changes at the hair salon, instant fashion change at your favorite clothing store, instant success by making the right investments, instant headache relief with the right medication. Instant! Instant! Instant!

First, learn to like yourself. If you don't like yourself, no one else will either. Take our perfect society with a grain of salt. With the right amount of money, time, and effort, cosmetic surgery, diet, and exercise, you too could have Hollywood perfection—but why would you want to? Be yourself and like yourself.

Personally speaking, I'm a few pounds overweight, my hair is getting thin, I don't wear all of the designer labels, and whenever I get the chance, I like to sit down to a breakfast of fried eggs, bacon, hash browns, and good old-fashioned toast made with white bread. But I have also learned to like myself.

Second, stop thinking in instant gratifications! It has been said it usually takes about 20 years to become an overnight success. Believe it! How often have you been disappointed by the results of the so-called instant fix? The perfect car didn't make heads turn as you drove down the road. It now takes you 20 more minutes of preparation time to keep that new hairstyle. You have been working out for three months and you have only lost 10 pounds.

Learn to like yourself, know it takes time, and, if necessary, become a realist. An optimist sees a glass of water as half full. A pessimist sees the same glass of water as half empty. A realist says the glass holding the water is too big.

Make goals! Give yourself the chance to have as much direction and purpose as possible!

LEADERSHIP

Every manager should have their title changed to leader. If we had more leaders, the problems associated with management would be nonexistent. Most of the problems associated with management are centered around people.

Somehow it became popular to be called manager, and titles were given out for every reason. These titles ranged from general manager, general sales manager, sales manager, and assistant manager to floor manager, department manager, and area manager. Each "manager" was responsible for managing people and their actions.

> It is possible to manage things, places, and events, but *never* people. You will, on the other hand, *always* be able to lead people.

Leader Characteristics

The theory of leadership has prompted the publication of many books and articles. They all highlight certain personal qualities, characteristics that seem to be universal among good leaders. These include:

- Trustworthy.
- Honest.
- Likes people.
- Happy
- Flexible.
- Logical.
- Straightforward.
- Allows others to lead.
- Organized.
- Open.
- Confident
- Good communicator.
- Positive attitude.
- Good listener.
- Sense of humor.
- Committed.
- Self-motivated.
- Develops.
- Decisive.
- Self-starter.

It is important to realize success lies within the leader, not within the job or title. The job or title won't make a good leader. Only the person in the job or title can do that. It comes from within, with skills that can be mastered.

Types of Leaders

There are two distinct types of leaders: the conductor and the technician. Both styles of leadership have pros and cons, but they share one common goal—they lead, not manage.

The conductor   This style of leadership is like an orchestra conductor—someone who combines the work and abilities of others to create a harmonious piece. These leaders are known for their organization and delegating skills. For this reason, the conductor is labeled a hands-off or nonparticipating leader. Conductors tend to delegate duties and projects rather than work on things themselves.

This style works best when dealing with large groups that then rely on a few key people. This allows the conductor to remain organized and continue to delegate.

In this style, however, not all associates are given an opportunity to grow and reach their potential. Often a conductor is hard to reach without going through a key associate.

The technician   This style of leadership is hands-on or participating. These individuals are the experts and prefer to handle everything themselves. They possess exceptional skills, and store policy and procedures knowledge. This style works best when the leader is working with uncommitted associates—those who just show up, do what is required, and go home.

A technician has the feeling of knowing all of the answers all of the time. Unfortunately, this feeling results in the technician withdrawing even further into self-sufficiency and totally neglecting staff development. The staff is essentially overmanaged (overled), and their professional growth is stunted.

As you have imagined, you will utilize both styles of leadership in the day-to-day operation of your store. During certain times of the day and with certain associates, you will be a conductor. Other times and other associates will require you to be a technician. Neither style is preferred, but be careful how each is used. Trying to conduct uncommitted associates will backfire. As well, if you try to do it all yourself without the assistance of your key people, they just may let you.

To be a good leader, you must master the personal qualities outlined in the previous pages. Which characteristics are the most important? They all are! If you really think about it, you can't be honest, confident, and happy yet disorganized and a poor listener with no sense of humor. The bad or indifferent skills will defeat the good skills. You have created a state of confusion.

The best way to learn good leadership skills is through practice and experience. Target those skills, like the list of strengths and weaknesses you read about earlier. Rate yourself by skills you now have and skills you want to acquire. As always, be specific and detailed. Then, concentrate on one skill at a time. Thoroughly master it before moving to the next. Also, develop a solid network of mentors—learn from the leaders you admire. If possible, ask questions about their experiences and management techniques. Don't attempt to imitate them, but create your own leadership style based on the positive qualities exhibited by others.

Even in the best of times, being in a position of leadership is emotionally challenging. Since you are ultimately responsible for your operation's performance and that of everyone connected to it, your task will be much easier and more rewarding if you know how to effectively lead your staff. You either propel yourself forward or hold yourself back. The power to succeed or fail is yours alone. Above all, be willing to do everything and anything you ask of your staff.

In conclusion, the previous pages have just touched on the topics. Take every opportunity you can to learn about yourself—your abilities, skills, and limitations. The better you know you, the easier it is to incorporate others into the store environment and its success.

Chapter Six

The Future Is Now

INTRODUCTION

T he overall success of your store is made up of the following percentages:

Location	6%
Products and/or services	4
Housekeeping/decor	3
Store hours	1
Home office/owner support	1
Policy/procedure	1
Associates	84
	100%

Your very existence depends on your ability as manager to find and maintain a top-notch sales and sales support force. I realize the above percentages will bruise a few egos. But reality is reality. The owners, home office personnel, president, vice presidents, buyers, accounting office, and human resources people wouldn't have their jobs if not for some online sales associate making the sales!

Now let's make these numbers even more frightening! For most retail operations, the lion's share of sales occur during the evenings (5 PM to 9 PM) and on the weekends (Saturday and Sunday). The actual percentages change from store to store, but overall, between 60 and 85 percent of total store sales occur during these hours and days. Typically, who is working the lion's share of these hours? You guessed it! The part-time sales associates. Then, when we factor in all of the stereotypes about the part-time associate (such as uncommitted, looking for a good time, uncaring, unmotivated, and unskilled), it really starts to make you wonder why you ever wanted to be a retail manager in the first place.

Are you scared yet? You should be! If not, read on. This part of the book will detail just three elements, but remember, over 80 percent of your success is focused in these three areas and your ability to master them.

As a quick note, I don't necessarily believe all of the so-called stereotypes mentioned before. These have been provided by managers in the industry—managers just like you. As well, keep in mind that your situation may dictate different approaches. The examples in the following pages should be considered guidelines for your personal (or store) policy adaptation.

Welcome to the three " 'ems": recruit 'em, motivate 'em, and develop 'em.

ASSOCIATE RECRUITING

The recruiting of good store associates is a continuous concern facing many retail managers today. It seems to always work like Murphy's law: when the economy is good and our sales are high, we can't find good staff members; when the economy is low and sales are off, we have an abundance of good people looking for an opportunity.

Let's look at the past 30 years and see what has changed. In the 1960s, many young people were attracted to the retail profession for part-time jobs. As well, with the expansion rate of the industry as a whole, retailers looked to young people to fill their needed positions. In reality, it was an employer's marketplace. The employer could pick and choose the best of the best to fill a position. The person would come into the store ready to contribute to its success.

In the 1970s, the retail industry enjoyed its fastest expansion in history in sheer numbers of locations. The industry now started to reverse itself, and during this time period, it became an employee's market. It was now employees' turn to pick and choose the best of the best. Retailers able to grab the very best associates were successful beyond their wildest expectations! Still, the people came into the stores very motivated, and their attitude seemed to be What can I do to help you? The 1970s produced hard-working people who needed their own independence, spending money, and college educations. The most important motivator seemed to be a start and a job recommendation. During the late 1970s, a college degree was almost an automatic hire.

The 1980s arrived. At first things were good, then they got bad, and finally downright ugly! During the early 80s, it was a strong employer's market. The first recession hit and times were tough; high interest rates, factory closings, and high rates of unemployment were common. In many locations, people would line up for hours just to have a chance to fill out an application. These people were well educated, and they brought with them many years of experience (remember Murphy's law).

As the job market worsened, the masses of people who would have normally entered the work force instead went to school. By the mid 1980s, the economy had turned itself around strongly. Now once again it was an employee's market. As many managers have communicated, this time period—1985 through 1990—brought a different person through their stores' front doors. Their attitude was one of What are you going to do for me?! They didn't have strong work ethics; in fact, most had no previous job experience.

For many of these people entering the work force during this time (the go-go years, as they are referred to), everything in life had been provided—the best designer clothing, cars, college educations, spending money, and more! I'm not saying that wanting to give children all of the things their parents never had was bad, but something was missing. Two of the extremes of this time period were shared with us. Unfortunately, both these case histories thought they were right. You decide. The first involved a young man whose father had given him a two-year-old Porsche to drive. He was angry with his father because he had to pay for the gas and insurance, and that's why he was working. The second involved a young lady who was a senior in high school and was forced to work to help support her monthly clothing expenses. As it was told, her parents would only provide her with a $1,000 *monthly* clothing allowance. If she wanted more, she had to earn her own money.

Please don't misunderstand. Not every person who came into the stores to apply for jobs carried things to these extremes, but an attitude was still present.

Thank goodness the 1990s came! Now, with everyone going to college and competition intense in the job market, it is once again returning to an employer's market. The young job applicants have realized the need for job experience to compete for that great and wonderful career they hope to someday have. Their attitude is once again What can I do for you? Be careful before you get too excited. The industry as a whole is still experiencing this overgrowth event. The future associate you want to hire just may have five or six offers on the table.

What does the year 2000 hold? There are many theories. Unfortunately, we will have to wait until that time to really tell.

As you have undoubtedly noticed, I have devoted many

pages to the part-time, young associate and past problems and concerns. Take a moment and reread this chapter's introduction, and then come back and read on.

Considerations

It's interesting how there are always two sides of every fence, two sides to every coin, and two different points of view.

A retail manager's point of view There aren't any good associates out there! They can't fill out job applications, they come into the stores dressed in shorts and T shirts, they bring in two or three friends, they are not self-motivated. It would be nice for a change to have a new associate ask for more responsibility and not wait for me to make them do something.

A potential associate's point of view Do they show me they care and are committed?! Why should I be committed to someone who isn't committed to me? What's wrong with my clothing? What's wrong with my hair? I have choices, and I don't have to work for you if I don't want to.

Let me offer some food for thought for both the manager and the potential associate.

Managers' food for thought Don't be too critical of the way people present themselves. They are probably not doing it out of spite or disrespect, they just don't know any better. No one has prepared them for picking up an application, how to dress for success, or even what to expect during an interview.

Be careful of your interviewing questions and what you really mean. When you ask about _____, do you really mean the following?

Self-motivated—can you go in the back room, find a dust rag and cleaner, and clean the shelves?

Confidence—can you run a vacuum cleaner and take out the trash?

Communication skills—can you talk to total strangers about our products, or will you just spend time with your friends on the phone?

Strengths—are you strong enough to carry the boxes of stock out to the sales floor and unpack them?

Please don't misunderstand. Many managers would do more for their associates, but when associates don't ask, after a while management feels they don't care.

Potential associates' and associates' food for thought   Prepare yourself! When you go in for the application, go in well prepared to fill it out, leave your friends at home, dress for the part, and above all, show the manager that you are committed. It's not the manager's responsibility to give you more opportunity. If you want it, ask for it! Remember, there will be times when your retail opportunity is not like the lifestyles of the rich and famous; it's not 8 to 5, weekends off, great pay, and a corporate jet to use for travel. It is weekends and evenings, minimum wages, very few benefits, and doing the least-liked jobs (stock work, cleaning, and dusting). But you will write your own job recommendation, and someday someone is going to ask, What did you do at your last job? Your response will either be Oh, not much or Sales! Customer service! Inventory control! Scheduling! Training! Marketing! and many other elements.

I will never argue the point that everyone associated with a retail store contributes to its success, no matter how big or small this contribution may seem. However, one factor of success stands alone, and I will argue this point until death!!! Nothing happens until a sale is made! The only person who can make the sale is the associate working one on one with the customer. Every salesperson will have a lasting effect on the store's success or its failure. Let's do some recruiting.

Murphy's Laws of Recruiting

- The person you believe to be your first and best choice for the job will be the first person you terminate.

- The person you believed would never last but gave a chance anyway (felt sorry for them or you needed a warm body on the sales floor) will turn out to be the best person you ever hired.

Sooner or later, people will learn how to answer the interview questions—and they will respond accordingly. Also, all it takes for a person to perform beyond expectations is to be given a chance and the right opportunity.

Two Other Important Factors

- Never rely on past experiences when recruiting! Don't compare new prospects with a past one-in-a-million person. Remember, such a person is one in a million.

- Recruiting is a full-time job! Resist the temptation to recruit only when you need a new associate. Train yourself to be constantly on the lookout for good people. You never know when one may show up and when a need may arise.

Your Last Two Thoughts

- Don't hire the best of the worst. Hire the best of the best! This is easier said than done, but if you don't like the existing applicants, start over! Somehow, we live in a world of justification: after all of your efforts have been completed, you will feel the need to hire someone just to justify your efforts. Don't! If necessary, start over! You don't have to justify every effort you take; you do, however, have to justify doing it right.

- Follow your company's policies and any and all state laws to a T! As silly as this may seem, these policies and laws are there to protect you from potential liability. In essence, if some law or policy on the books requires you to wear a straw hat with a banana attached to it, you had better do it! This may sound outlandish, but have you ever read the codes concerning the hiring of people? They will amaze you!

Recruiting Steps

First, get prepared Lay things out on paper to give yourself some direction. Try to avoid setting too many conditions, looking for the ideal candidate. Doing so will only add to your frustrations if your perfect expectations are not met. Look for the basics, including:

- Male/female.
- Ages—approximate.
- Experience, or lack of it.

During merchant seminars, I often ask this question: Would you hire me? Immediately, several hands will go up and I will hear a loud yes. When I ask one or two of these people why, they always respond, Experience! Then, I ask those who didn't raise their hands, Why wouldn't you hire me? They also respond, Experience!

This debate has raged for years and years. It's like the debate of which came first, the chicken or the egg. Both have their positives and negatives.

Obviously, our ideal applicant would have many years of experience, skills, abilities, a positive outlook, and no bad habits. In essence, each will require your time and energy, not a shortcut. And we have all driven with someone who knows a shortcut, haven't we?

Experienced

Positive	Negative
Selling skills	Set in ways
Has seen things	Bad habits
Time savings	Waste time butting heads

Inexperienced

Positive	Negative
Not set in ways	No selling skills
No bad habits	Very green
Train them as you want	Many hours of time

Finally, it is often said we recruit people with a mirror image of ourselves. This can be good and bad. Remember, you have strengths and weaknesses, and a new associate will have strengths and weaknesses. Obviously, if you can add new dimension to your staff, do so.

Second, provide a general job description This is mostly for yourself. A short, basic job description includes the whos, whats, whens, wheres, and whys. This may encompass:

- Sales.
- Customer service.
- Cash register operations.
- Merchandising.
- Visual merchandising.
- Inventory control.
- Customer problems.
- Stock work.
- The usual cleaning/maintenance.

Third, hours Spell them out! Part-time, full-time, days, evenings, weekends. Put it all down on paper and see where the new associate will fit in.

Fourth, final, and most important: What are you going to provide and/or do for the new associate besides money?
This is going to create the new associate's loyalty and commitment to you and your business. Imagine for just a moment that you have found the perfect person for your job opening. In a nutshell, you can provide for this person's financial needs—their hourly salary. How many other stores can provide the same financial package or a better one? If all you provide is money, the new associate will most likely leave you for the first better money option. You must offer more than the money to keep their loyalty and commitment. These offerings may include:

- Opportunity—promotions from part-time to full-time; full-time to manager trainee; manager trainee to assistant manager; assistant manager to manager.
- Company transfers.
- Job recommendations within company guidelines.
- The business education—selling, motivating, merchandising, customer service, scheduling, marketing, and inventory control, just to name a few options.
- Benefits—insurance, profit-sharing, vacations, company savings plans.
- Incentives—bonuses, commissions, perks.
- Discounts on purchases.
- A headstart into the job market with experience.

In any event, you can offer more than money, and this may be what is required to keep the associate.

The search The successful search for new associates will encompass many traditional and nontraditional approaches. You will often find yourself using a combination of methods.

Advertising Advertising in a local newspaper or trade paper is still the most used method of finding new people. In this method, you will probably talk with and view the largest number of applicants. The drawback is that you will also talk with many people you would never hire.

Help wanted signs seem to have grown in popularity over the past few years. Sometimes they simply say help wanted, other times they are fancy. Both are also advertising. If you "advertise" for a position most states require you to give out an application to each and every person who responds.

If possible, your advertising message should include a brief job description, days or times when applications are taken, and to whom the applicant should apply.

As a side note, I do not recommend placing help wanted signs in your store windows. They often look cheap and tacky, and they detract from your image. If you want the help wanted signs, make them in the image of your store (perhaps a plaque made out of wood and brass with hanging "position" brass pieces that can be changed as the need requires). Place this by the desk area, not in the front window. Such signs in the windows will do two things for you: first, they advertise to your customers that you have help problems; second, they put out a welcome mat for shoplifters. Over the past few years, several shoplifting rings have been broken up by the police, who discovered that shoplifting rings specifically target stores with help wanted signs in the windows. These signs tell shoplifters they have a greater chance of getting away with the crime because of low floor coverage.

Associations Associations are a great place to find good people. Business memberships and relations will help you, if you just ask and let your needs be known.

Current staff Many managers have found great success by simply asking their current staff if they know of someone who would be interested in an opportunity. Know going into this method that a problem could be created: if your current associates recommend a friend, now you have two friends working together. Some managers even place a bounty on the hiring of a recommendation: $20, $25, and even $50 will have your associates bringing in people.

Schools and colleges   This could be your single best resource for good employees. High schools, trade schools, community colleges, junior colleges, and four-year schools are full of people just waiting to fill your needs. Concentrate your efforts on the counselors, placement directors, teachers, and coaches—always speaking with them personally! The success of such recruiting efforts depends on how well you present yourself and your company. Provide as much information concerning the company, the opportunity, and yourself as possible. The secret to using this source is that the counselors, placement directors, teachers, and coaches know of specific situations of which you aren't aware. They are also a great source of recommendations.

A new twist to the schools and colleges is the use of direct-mail postcards, as shown in the illustration.

Obtain a mailing list of students at local high schools, community colleges, and four-year institutions. Create a postcard as below. You may receive good applicants.

ANY STORE
123 Easy Street
Anytown, Any State 12345

    SUSAN STUDENT
    456 Main Street
    Anytown, Any State 12345

WE MAY HAVE A POSITION FOR YOU!
If you're interested in EXTRA MONEY
. . . NEW RESPONSIBILITY . . . A HEAD
START . . . We're interested in you!
Please call _____ to set up
a time for us to get together.

    Sincerely yours,

    Signature
    Title

These can be mailed or sent to specific groups, such as:

- **Drama Clubs**   • **Athletic Teams**
- **Cheerleaders**   • **Band Members**

Customers   How about customers? They already know and trust you and your store. They may also have sons and daughters who would make perfect additions to your staff.

Bulletin boards   Bulletin boards at factories, apartment buildings, and churches are another great way to communicate your needs. Remember, you never know from where a good associate will come.

Headhunters   And last but certainly not least—the art of headhunting! How often have you been impressed by a store associate working for another company? Chances are, many times. You may have even said, I wish they were working for me. Well, steal them!

Many managers have problems with this recruiting method, but it can be done with tact and grace where everyone wins. If you are not comfortable with plain old stealing, talk to the wanted person's managers first. Often you will be surprised at the outcome. Their supervisors will tell you that they welcome your interest, they don't have the opportunities you do, the person is already looking for a change, perhaps you could share the person, just to name a few responses. Obviously, you could also be told a very loud and strong no. In either event, you warned them. So go ahead and steal them! Always remember, over 80 percent of your success lies within your staff. Your choice is to continue to wish upon a star or to take action.

As a final note to the search, treat all applicants in a friendly, congenial manner, whether they are considered for employment or not. They are still a customer or a potential customer.

Applications   Your companies and/or local stationery stores will provide what is legally correct. As everyone's application blanks could be different, take a moment to review the papers with applicants before they fill them out. And, when they are done, review the papers again and have the applicants fill in any blank spaces. The point is, give the applicants a chance, especially if you are working with someone very inexperienced. Yours may be the first application they ever saw, let alone filled out.

Often, inexperienced applicants will need your help. If they have never had a job, ask them about baby- or pet-sitting, house-sitting, lawn care, paper routes, school organizations, and clubs or networks. Give them a chance; they could just turn out to be the one-in-a-million person you were looking for.

Never, never, never, write on, attach to, or staple anything other than a resume to any application. If you do, it becomes a permanent part of the file! Many a manager and company have found themselves in serious legal trouble for doing just this. Keep your notes (good or bad) on a separate sheet of paper.

It's unfortunate but true, the application doesn't give us much information other than statistics—name, address, phone, school background, past job information, and references. For this reason, many managers immediately talk with applicants before they leave to get a better feel for the person. If this feeling is positive, set the application in a stack for interviews; if not, set the application in a stack for further review, before you file it away. In essence, give every application a second ''once-over'' before you file it away (remember Murphy's law).

Interviewing   Interviews can be the most stressful things applicants do! Put yourself in their shoes. You would enjoy a relaxed, one-on-one conversation; so would the applicant. Often, managers will turn up the heat and do anything to make an applicant squirm just a little bit more. Don't do it! You are not there to create problems, you are there to solve problems.

The following interview questions will give you a guideline from which to begin the process. As you notice, the first questions under personal evaluation are very light in nature. They get progressively harder and more to the point.

Personal Evaluation

1. What is the hardest thing you have ever done?
2. What do you feel has been your greatest accomplishment?
3. What has been your greatest disappointment?
4. What are your pet peeves, the things that upset you most?
5. What is your standard for your own success?
6. What do people most often criticize you for?
7. What do you most often criticize others for?
8. What factors in your past have contributed most to your development?
9. What factors acted as handicaps to your development?
10. In general, how would you describe yourself?
11. In which areas do you feel you would like to develop yourself further?
12. What are your long-range goals and objectives?
13. What kinds of situations or circumstances make you feel tense or nervous?
14. What do you regard to be your outstanding qualities?
15. What do you regard to be some of your shortcomings?
16. What kind of people upset you most readily?

Attitude toward the Job

1. What reservations do you have about this job?
2. What do you think should be the principal qualifications for this job?

3. What do you think you will like most (least) about this job?

4. What do you think will be the hardest part of this job?

5. Other than technical training, in what ways can the company help you in this job?

6. What are some of the things in a job that are most important to you?

7. What do you think is likely to make the difference between success and failure in this position?

8. If hired, how do you visualize your future with this company?

9. What other types of positions are you currently seeking or considering?

10. How does this position compare with others you may now be considering?

11. How did you decide to apply for this position?

Education

1. What courses did you get the most out of?

2. What courses gave you the most difficulty?

3. What did you like least about school?

4. What did you enjoy most about school?

5. Describe your best teacher.

6. What kind of person was your worst teacher?

7. What special techniques would you use if you were a teacher?

8. How do you think school contributed to your development?

9. What were your work plans at the time of graduation?

10. Tell me about the ways you spent your summers while in school.

11. Tell me about your extracurricular activities.

12. What determined your choice of major?

13. Why did you choose the particular school that you did?

Work Experience

1. How did you get your job with the XYZ Company?

2. Describe the (*last employer*) company as a place to work.

3. What would you rather have done more of in your last job?

4. What aspects of your last job did you like least?

5. If you could have made one suggestion to management in your last job, what would it have been?

6. Tell me about the best (worst) boss you ever had.

7. What do you feel you gained from your association with the XYZ Company?

8. How do you think your present (past) supervisor would describe you?

9. What was the most difficult part of your last job?

10. What were some of the things about which you and your supervisor disagreed?

11. In what ways have your past jobs prepared you for greater responsibilities?

12. Describe an upsetting experience that took place on your last job.

13. What kind of position would you like to hold in five years?

14. What were the major problems you encountered on your last job, and how did you solve them?

15. How do you feel about the progress you have made with your present (last) employer?

You don't have to ask every question on these lists, but use them as a guideline to continue the conversation.

Many managers have found success during the interviewing process with a back door situation. The back door method allows you to create a situation with which to see two things at once: first, how the applicants would react, and second, if they would do it on their own. It may look like the following:

> How to handle a customer complaint: Let's say you have been hired for the position and it's your first day on the job. It's Saturday, a customer walks in with a problem, and you are waiting on him. I'm busy with a customer, the assistant manager has the day off, and you get to take care of the customer. How would you handle it?

Amazingly, most applicants will be concentrating so hard on saying the right thing about the methods of satisfying the customer that they won't know your hidden agenda (in this example, will they try on their own—right or wrong—to take the initiative, or will they wait for you?).

Remember, there are professional interviewees out there. If every answer to every question is too perfect, be ready with some back door situations to see what is really taking place.

The magic of the interviewing process is that you control it! After a few minutes of getting to know the person, if your gut feeling says it's time to stop, stop! If things are going well, continue. As mentioned before, however, remember Murphy's law: don't stop too quickly.

If the applicants have survived, now is the time to give them some information, including:

- Company background.
- Business philosophy, guidelines, and perspectives.

- Your background.
- Your personality.
- The job details.

Now let the applicants know you will be checking their past job references and any personal references.

References   It has almost gotten to the point where this is a complete waste of time. Examine what has taken place. The legal problems associated with giving job recommendations have forced almost every company to only provide the following: yes, the person worked here from _____ to _____. Her salary was _____. And, if you are really lucky, the reference will tell you if they would or would not rehire the applicant. This legal problem has gone so far as to exclude the good job recommendations as well. Many cases pending in the court system are referenced to good reports. If you received a stellar reference from a past employer, you would think this is great. You would hire the person, and if he doesn't work out, you terminate him. Someone has to pay! Let's sue the company for giving out a false report. You may even assume the company set you up. It was trying to get rid of the person in the first place, and it found you to take care of the problem associate.

References pose different problems. Do applicants pull references off the street? No! They are handpicked for their ability to help the applicant achieve the goal—a job. Fortunately, with a little probing you can get more information. But don't be too surprised at what you hear. One of the best stories still told is of a manager who was talking with an applicant's reference. At first, the person sounded great! Then, as the conversation continued, the manager found out that the applicant owed the reference a great deal of money was trying to help the person land a job in hopes of collecting on the debt.

Many companies have now resorted to administering tests of qualities like personality, honesty, and philosophy to gain information about the job applicant. Can you blame them? Keep in mind that these tests, like the interview questions, can be answered perfectly with some practice. If a test asked you the following question, how would you answer it?

> If a customer overpaid you for a purchase by $5.00, what would you do?
>
> - Keep it for lunch money.
> - Put it in the cash drawer for extra profit.
> - Give it back to the customer.

It won't make you long to figure out how to answer this question and others like it correctly to get the job.

Right about now, you should be saying to yourself, hold it for just a minute, do you mean that I have to worry about Murphy's Laws? More than eighty percent of my success is brought about by good associates—but they may be uncommitted, they may be professional interviewees, and I can't really get a check on past jobs or rely on references? How do I know that anyone is the right person for me? The answer to your concerns is a very loud *you don't!* Remember when, in the introduction to this chapter, I asked Are you scared yet? If you weren't then, you most likely are now.

There isn't a magic formula for finding and selecting the right associates for your job openings. You must rely on your instincts and gut reaction to hire them or not. As you well know, there aren't any guarantees with recruiting the right associates. Your instantaneous judging may not always be fair or accurate. It will take time before you instinctively know what is right.

Selection Best-case scenario would be finding five perfectly suitable applicants for one position. Normally, this just isn't the case. After swimming through a pile of applications, if you have one, you should still hold a second interview to confirm your feelings. If, after the second interview, your feelings aren't the same, start over! Don't make the mistake of hiring someone—anyone—just to have a warm body on the sales floor. Hiring the best of the worst isn't worth the trouble it will cause in the long run.

Hiring the wrong person will do tremendous damage to your operation, such as:

- Damage to sales.
- Damage to customer relations.
- Increase in customer service problems.
- Decrease in the morale of other associates.
- Wasted money—people aren't cheap.
- Wasted time—how much an hour are you worth?

Be prepared to start over if necessary! After all of your time and energy was spent, don't hire someone—anyone—just to justify your effort. Once you have made your choice, get the new associate back into the store as soon as possible.

Job offer   When you have determined who you would like to hire, it's time to extend the job offer. Your offer should contain three elements.

1. Recheck   This step includes rechecking with the new associate for problems or conflicts, such as transportation, outside activities, and prior commitments. Just because a new associate has outside activities or prior commitments doesn't make a problem, but be aware of things. If, for example, your new associate is going to play on the basketball team, know he will be at practice until 5 PM every afternoon. Obviously, he wouldn't be able to start his work shift until 5:30 at the soonest, most likely not until 6.

2. Job description   Include a brief outline of what the new associate will be doing. This could be identical to what you did for yourself during the planning stages, such as:

- Sales.
- Customer service.
- Cash register.
- Merchandising.
- Inventory control.
- Customer problems.
- Stock work.
- Visual merchandising.
- Usual cleaning and maintenance.

If possible, provide this job description in writing.

3. Compensation and benefits   Spell out the compensation package and any and all opportunities the new associate will and could receive, such as:

- Salary and/or hourly pay.
- Commissions, bonuses.
- Overtime.
- Benefits—health care, profit-sharing, savings plans, vacations, and purchase discounts.
- Opportunity—promotions within the company, transfers, job recommendations (per company policy), the business education, a head start into the job market.

Once again, provide this information in writing for the new associate.

Many managers have great success by providing the opportunity part of the compensation package in the form of an actual agreement between employee and employer. This may be structured as shown in the illustration.

As you can see, the agreement on page 210 covers both the new associate and you, the manager. Resist the temptation to make this agreement just for the associate. Remember, this is a two-way street in terms of a commit-

Agreement

I, _____, the manager/owner of_____
_____, do hereby commit to _____, associate
of_____. And, I,_____,
associate of_____do hereby commit to_____
_____ , the manager/owner, of _____
the following:

_____, manager/owner.
I will always be honest and up-front with you concerning information
about job descriptions, duties, responsibilities, schedules, reviews
and expectations.

I will work to provide for you as much information, education, and
knowledge as possible. This will include sales and customer service
and other business/retail knowledge.

I will take responsibility for you and your development as it fits
into the store's objectives for success.

I will provide job recommendations and references about our existing
and/or past relationship whenever and wherever the company policy
and regulations allow me to do so.

_____, associate
I will always be honest and up-front with you concerning my abilities
to perform job duties, responsibilities, and schedules.

I pledge 100% of my support to the company during my time and I will
seek new ways to make it more successful.

I will perform my job to the best of my abilities, even if I dislike
the task.

I will work on my own to gain new knowledge, understanding, and
perspectives about my position and the company.

I will take responsibility for my words and actions, even if it means
criticism of my performance.

I understand that whatever recommendation and reference the company
is able to give me I wrote from my performance.

Dated this_____ day of _____,19_____

_____   _____
Manager/Owner   Associate

ment. You are committed to the associate, and the associate is committed to you!
Remember:

- Remain flexible.
- Every associate represents new challenges, problems, and successes.
- Don't be in a hurry.
- Don't hire the best of the worst.
- And your work has just begun; good associates are made, not born; their success depends on you, your leadership, and your commitment!

ASSOCIATE MOTIVATION

This is still a great argument! Often it is asked, Why do I have to motivate them when just having this job should be motivation enough? The answer and truth to this question is this: if you don't motivate your associates, someone else will. Motivation is absolutely fundamental to the practice of management and leadership.

Once you have a good staff, motivate them to greatness! The first part of associate motivation is nothing more than common sense—doing things, acting a certain way, or speaking certain words in a positive atmosphere. The second part of motivation will break down your common sense to one-on-one motivation.

Positive Motivators

- *Recognize all accomplishments.* Your associates need to feel important and that they are contributing to the success of the operation, regardless of their position. Let them know when you appreciate them or when they have done something good.

- *Encourage them to set goals.* Let them have confidence with the I-can-do-it-too philosophy.
- *Clarify expectations.* Your associates need to know where they stand and what is expected. When they reach your expectations, they feel good.
- *Individualize your supervision.* To maximize motivation, you must treat people as individuals. While some people need close supervision, others do not. Don't overmanage, yet give guidance and help.
- *Exhibit confidence in your associates.* Confidence results in positive performance. A positive performance results in the associate seeking more. More creates confidence.
- *Establish a climate of trust and open communication.* Motivation is at its highest in organizations that encourage trust and openness. Trust your associates and let your door be open anytime.
- *Listen to your associates.* They will share their joys, fears, accomplishments, and failures, if you let them. People feel important when someone listens.

Negative De-Motivators

Positive motivators are the golden rule. However, the goal in motivating is not merely to motivate but also to refrain from actions that de-motivate. Certain negative factors are so powerful, they can destroy every positive thing we do. These negative de-motivators are not being shown to you so you have a new destructive tool to demoralize your staff. Often managers will say, My staff is not motivated! When the manager is questioned further, we discover it's really the manager who is de-motivating the staff, not motivating them. The following are the most common de-motivating mistakes made by managers and store leaders.

1. Never belittle an associate in front of others. Your associates may have self-doubts about their abilities, but they don't like others to share that opinion. Don't talk about an associate's shortcomings in front of others.

2. Never fail to give your associates attention when they need it. The problem may seem trivial to us, but if it affects their performance, you had better take it seriously.

3. Don't show your staff your only concern is yourself. Don't be selfish and manipulate the staff for your own purposes. Your staff won't mind helping you achieve your goals as long as you demonstrate you will return the favor.

4. Don't play favorites. It's truly amazing how the mind works. If you have been giving a lot of attention to one particular staff member, the others may feel threatened. Trying to avoid playing favorites is a difficult challenge. It's our human nature to be drawn to the good people, but it's crucial to give everyone an equal chance.

5. Don't fail to help your associates grow. Let them see and do as much as they want. If someone wants to know the ins and outs of the scheduling process, share it. If someone wants to know about recruiting, share your knowledge. Don't hold good people back, even if it means they will be promoted or transferred. Help your staff to grow beyond your immediate grasp.

6. Never show up the staff. It's embarrassing for associates to have a manager show off at their expense! Of course you can ring up the sale faster, check in merchandise better, and create a more dazzling display—that's why you are the store manager/store leader and get paid the big money. Let the associates learn to do their job, and they will.

7. Don't lower your standards. Lowering your standards for one or two associates will only bring down the entire staff. Don't lower, rather raise the subpar people.

8. Don't put off making a decision. Make a decision as

quickly as possible—when you have all of the information to make a decision. Sometimes it's necessary to put off a decision until all of the facts are in place, but tell them why. If you procrastinate, you can be sure your associates will!

Once again, these are commonsense rules. When you really examine the de-motivators, you will find yourself using them not out of spite or on purpose, but because of your anger with a situation. As always, anger is an emotion, and emotions are best kept out of management and leadership.

Constructive Criticism

Criticism as a motivator? Yes! One of the best things managers can do is give their associates direction and standards. Criticism in the right dose and provided on a constructive basis is the key to success. The constructive criticism points out not only what is wrong but also how to improve; it's a confidence builder.

1. Don't let hostilities build up. If something is bothering you, get it out!

2. Choose the correct time to criticize. The best time is in private—just you and the associate, never in front of other people. Many managers find it helpful to leave the store with the associate, at break or lunch time, if possible.

3. Express confidence! The hardest criticism is easier to take, accept, and apply when it's given with reassurance on improved performance in the future.

4. Criticize one point at a time. If more than one area deserves attention, take it one point at a time. Don't criticize—criticize—criticize. Rather, criticize, rebuild, criticize, rebuild.

5. Offer specific advice. Offer tools, knowledge, past experiences to improve. This makes the criticism truly constructive.

6. Don't incorporate the words *always* or *never* into criticism. These words imply every time, and this is simply not true.

- You *always* leave the lights on.
- You *never* clean up after yourself.
- You are *always* trying to change the schedule.
- You *never* ring up layaway sales right.

When you use the words *always* or *never* in criticism, it immediately puts up a defensive wall between you and the accused. They will remember sometime, someplace when they didn't do what you accused them of doing: That's not true! On June 17, 1993, at 2:09 PM, I did it right! Expect a defensive response to an always or never accusation.

7. Don't beat around the bush. Get to the point as fast as possible. It's torture to know a criticism is coming and to anticipate the pain. In many cases, this awkward delay is worse than the actual criticism!

8. Use positives, not negatives. Rebuild your associates with positive statements; offer them an I know you'll do better! Don't leave them with negative doubt.

And last, but certainly not least!

9. Remember your image as the leader of the store. If you are perceived as a strong leader, expect your associates to imitate you. This imitation will be of both your good traits and bad traits. Criticism carries with it a message about the critic—do you have double standards? One for you and one for the associates? If you criticize an associate for taking a long lunch, and your last lunch was over two hours, your image has been damaged.

One-on-One

Everything covered thus far has been common sense and theory—philosophy. But one-on-one associate motivation is quite different.

One-on-One
Motivation

✓ **Become a great listener**
✓ **Treat each individually**

Recognition
Opportunist
Belonging
Security

You must master the following two areas to become a great one-on-one motivator.

1. Become a great listener Listening to your associates will tell you everything you need to know. (Just like listening to the customer will tell you everything you need to know.) Your associates will tell you what is emotionally important to them. Don't confuse this with what is important to you, the store, or your company. Look at things through their eyes. Your associates may have two or three emotional switches, both work related and personal related. These emotional switches are the reasons they perform their job for you. If you turn off the switch, they won't perform very well. Likewise, if you turn up the switch, they will do even better.

These emotional switches can change on a daily basis—one day, it's a raise; the next, a new car; the next, more responsibility, travel, awards, promotions, or transfers.

Keep in touch with your associates, every chance you get! The more you know about them, the easier it will be to motivate them one on one.

2. Learn to treat each associate individually All too often we try to find and use one motivating tool for all of our associates. This isn't realistic. But day in and day out, companies, stores, and managers still believe there is such a tool. This tool is money. In some instances, money is the motivator. In most instances, however, money is the catalyst for producing the real reason for doing a good job. There are four basic reasons for doing a good job. All of your associates will fit into at least one of these groups. And don't be surprised if they fit into multiple group classifications.

Recognition These people like to be recognized for their efforts; they like awards, certificates, letters of commendation, listing in the company bulletins, and monetary rewards if they are part of a contest, promotion, or event.

Opportunist These people are seeking a chance to advance; they like promotions, transfers, new responsibility, educational programs, and new knowledge.

Belonging These people like to be a part of the group: sales clubs (top 5, top 10), company functions, responsibilities as long as others join in, health clubs, and organized sporting activities.

Security These people like to be safe and secure. They like pension plans, savings programs, retirement plans, stock options, and CDs.

Now that you have become a great listener and know how to categorize their desires (and once again the emphasis is on their desires), you are ready to motivate them one on one.

Let's assume the following emotional switches for your staff to be true:

Bill—education and promotion to store manager.

Susan—number one in sales and a new car.

Tim—early retirement.

Karen—travel with groups.

Jim—finish his education.

Diane—amateur photography and savings account for a once-in-a-lifetime vacation.

Now that we have the emotional switches for each associate (learned by listening), we can begin to motivate. First, imagine a sales contest in which each associate will receive a $100 bonus at the end of the month if the store's goal is achieved. This one's easy. Just translate the money into something important for each associate. They may be as follows:

Bill—Thank you for helping to lead the staff last month during the contest. You have demonstrated some very good qualities, qualities you will need when you have your store. Oh, and by the way, here is the $100 bonus—go treat yourself.

Susan—Once again, you lead the staff in sales! Great job! Here is the $100 bonus; you're just that much closer to that new car.

Tim—Here is your $100 bonus. How is it going to be invested? Great job last month!

Karen—Here is an extra $100 for your upcoming trip. Great job last month!

Jim—Here is your $100 bonus for doing a great job last month. As a student, you will find good use for it, I'm sure.

Diane—Great job last month! Here is your $100 bonus. Are you going to buy that new camera lens, or save it?

All you have done is turn the prize, perk, or bonus into something important to each associate. For most managers, motivating their associates like this is easy with the perk ($100 bonus). Now take away the perk, and how would you motivate them one on one?

This is actually easier than it sounds! To continue to motivate them, remember their emotional switches. By constantly remembering your associates' switches, you can remind them by simply talking about their lives.

Bill—talk about him taking over his own store, how it may be the same or different, or how he may do things.

Susan—ask her how she will remain number one in sales and about the new car she desires.

Tim—ask him about investments.

Jim—ask him about his schooling and what's happening.

Diane—ask her about photography, about her desire for the once-in-a-lifetime vacation.

In essence, show your interest in your associates and what's important to them, and they will show interest in what's important to you—the store's success.

As you will notice, virtually everything thus far has been good, positive, and confirming. What about using fear to motivate the staff? Don't do it! Trying to scare your associates into doing a better job will further disintegrate a bad situation. Fear triggers a defense mechanism in almost every person. After you have exhausted all positive motivating methods, it may be necessary to terminate an employee. There is no disgrace in discharging an associate who is incapable of functioning at an acceptable level of performance. Your store can not be all things to all people, and not all people are equipped to fit in. If things have gotten to the point of anger and frustration save yourself the time and additional trouble—terminate the situation.

Remember:

• Use common sense.
• Avoid negative situations.

- Use constructive criticism.
- Relate one on one every chance you get.

ASSOCIATE DEVELOPMENT

Consider the following situation and the two options at the end.

> Imagine you have just left for a badly needed vacation, two weeks of fun and sun lying on the beaches. Your store is left in the capable hands of your assistant manager and the rest of your staff, two full-time associates and three part-time people. Four days into your trip, you receive a phone call from the store—an emergency. The assistant manager has broken her leg playing softball and will be in the hospital for the next three weeks. You now have two options. They may or may not be a choice.

Option one: You must pack up and return to the store immediately!

Option two: You stay put and enjoy the rest of your vacation while the remaining associates run the operation.

The only difference between option one and option two is that option two says you have trained and developed your staff to take over in any condition.

Unfortunately, many companies and managers believe nothing happens unless the manager is there. This theory is very unrealistic! If the manager is there all of the time— Monday through Friday, 9 AM to 9 PM; Saturday from 9 AM to 9 PM; and Sunday from noon until 5 PM—this manager is burned out and is overmanaging the operation. In essence, this manager has stunted the growth of the staff.

Thus far, everything you need to make your staff into a team operation has been provided—crisis control, delegation, sales management, sales plans, stress management, time management, goals, recruiting, and motivation. You possess the knowledge to lead your staff and store into greatness. The secret is to pass on as much as you know to your people. This is associate development: the art of developing your staff to do anything and everything and to work together as a team!

Have a plan! Even if it is a handwritten outline, it's a start. The more complete and detailed the plan is, the better it is.

The secret of becoming a great manager is not working 77 hours a week and then burning yourself out. Rather, it is to incorporate and develop your staff into their full potential.

Often managers will confuse development with training. Training is the *what* of a thing and *how*. Training your associates is like creating a robot—performance is achieved through repetition (such as, ringing up sales on the cash register). An associate will improve and be faster the more often the task is repeated. Development, on the other hand, incorporates the *what* and *how* of training but does it one better by adding the all important *why*! Through development, we create a complete picture of understanding.

Don't forget *why*! Remember growing up and being asked or told to do something by your parents? Being curious, you would undoubtedly ask, why? How many times did your parents respond, Because I asked or told you to, that's why. Are you going to simply train your staff, or are you going to develop them?

You are no longer a trainer. You must become a developer!

Have a Plan

A plan is a course of action and directions to guide yourself and your staff through virtually every element of your operation. Several years ago, it became popular to have a specific job description. This just isn't possible in a retail environment. One minute, you are selling; the next, motivating; the next, another customer; the next, filling out reports; the next . . . the next . . . the next. Resist the temptation to develop people part way, which often happens with part-time people. Be willing to take everyone all the way, or not at all.

Break your plan into time elements. This may be done weekly, bi-weekly, monthly, or every 60 days. Next, fill in each time element with jobs, duties, tasks—the *whats*. Your plan may take only a few weeks or months to complete with each associate, or it may take a year or longer. It is still correct to allow your staff to develop at their own pace; don't push and don't hold back. Remember to make your number one priority—sales—the lead element to your plan. Your plan may look like the following example (I have chosen one-month time periods):

Month One

Product knowledge.

Sales knowledge.

Cash register operation.

Methods of sale—cash, checks, credit.

Month Two

Product knowledge.

Sales knowledge.

Sales plans.

Weekly (bi-weekly, monthly) sales reports.

Merchandise displays.

Layaway follow-up.

Month Three

Product knowledge.

Sales knowledge.

Checking in merchandise.

Opening and closing procedures.

Scheduling.

Conduct first sales meeting.

Month Four . . . Month Five . . . Month Six . . . and so on.

Evaluate Your Staff

Once you have your plan laid out on paper, include your staff in the system. It will work best if you make a copy of your plan for each associate and simply find out where they are now. Use a system of check-offs as you evaluate each person. By knowing your staff's abilities and where they stand now, you will once again gain new direction. Enlist your staff to help direct your efforts. Have them evaluate themselves to tell you where they are.

Attach the *how to* to your list of *whats*. Take each job, duty, element, or task from your list of *whats* and attach the *how to* to them. The *how to* is nothing more than instructions, policy and procedures manuals, handouts, company policies, sales materials, and so on. Make it easy for the associate to do the job.

Attach the *why*. Communication and understanding of the complete picture are the critical elements to making your development plan work! Become a true developer. Don't say Because I told you to. And this will be the key element of success as you introduce your staff to the idea. Tell them *why* you are developing them! The *why* is the effect, result, benefit, influence, and impact each element has on the store and on them. If you don't have a full understanding of these *whys*, find out for yourself and then pass them along.

Examples of the *what, how,* and *why* process are as follows:

What—product knowledge.

How—store manuals; manufacturers' brochures; labels and care tags; boxes; instruction manuals; the look, feel, smell, and touch of the products.

Why—communication to the customer—features and benefits, knowledge, sell correct products to meet customer demands, answer questions, and determination of quality and value.

What—layaway follow-up.

How—review the layaway file and separate into current, 30 days past due, 60 days past due, and return to stock. Make follow-up phone calls and/or send notices to all past-due accounts. Return to stock all unwanted merchandise for immediate sale.

Why—cash flow; returned merchandise is now ready to sell; additional customer contacts; and keep our customers current.

Associate Evaluations

Evaluate your associates at the end of each time frame before they move to the next. Again, let them develop at their own pace, but don't let them move to new elements until they have mastered the current opportunities. For the most part, you don't need to conduct a lengthy, time-consuming evaluation. They can usually be completed in 5, 10, or 15 minutes at the most. The decision to move to the next stage should be left up to the associates. However, let them know that they will be called on to perform those jobs, duties, elements, and tasks, and if they are not done up to standard, it's a direct reflection on them. Don't push them forward until they are ready, but don't hold them back.

When you acquire a new associate, remember to start at the beginning and incorporate your other associates in the development process; let them become developers as well.

In previous chapters, you were given the opportunity to see the management and leadership process up close. Essential Skills took you to the beginning. Management Self-Evaluation gave you a great look at knowing yourself. And The Future Is Now has concentrated on the importance of your staff—find 'em, motivate 'em, and develop 'em.

Within your management environment, seek new knowledge every chance you get. Try, experiment, and test. No other profession in the world is as forgiving as retail. You can make a mistake, change direction, try new ideas, fall flat on your face, stand up and laugh at yourself, and go on. The crucial element is that you always remember to manage things, places, and events—and you lead people!

As before, don't put this material on management away. Use it! Share it with your associates. Help everyone in your organization to improve.

Unfortunately, space did not exist to incorporate many concerns you will face today as a manager. In the following pages, you will find specific questions and answers. Keep in mind, these answers may not work exactly as provided, but they will give you a starting point.

Questions and Answers

The following are specific questions and answers you will most likely face sometime in your career as a manager. The answers provided in some cases are but some of many possible solutions.

1. HOW DO I TERMINATE AN EMPLOYEE?

This is undoubtedly one of the least-liked management duties. But the fact of the matter is, it must be done on occasion. Often the manager will feel worse than the employee being terminated. The reason for this feeling is simple: the manager feels she has somehow failed. Keep in mind, you and your store cannot be all things to all people, and all people will not fit into your store.

First, ensure you have covered all requirements necessary to protect yourself and your store, including company policies and/or state laws. Then do one better than is required. For example, if your company policy requires three written corrective reviews before you can terminate, complete four. If a state law requires you to complete two of something, complete three; protect yourself and your company, and you also give the employee every chance possible.

If the final result is to terminate the employee, you must do it. Take out the emotion and use logic only. Have your reasons for termination available. Sit down with the associate face to face and confront the situation. Your opening conversation may sound like this:

> John, after careful review of your situation, your past performance reviews, and where things are now, I have come to the determination that our operation is not your cup of tea. In all reality, you can't be happy either with this constant stress hanging over your head. At this point, I feel it's best to sever our relationship. You can get on with other opportunities for which you may be better suited.

In this example, termination for nonperformance, you will often find the employees are just as relieved about being terminated as you are about terminating them.

Terminations for other causes are sometimes easier to perform. These reasons may include employee theft, breaking a company policy or rule, or misrepresentation or false information on an employment application. It's unfortunate that these causes for termination occur, but they do for various reasons.

Sit face to face with the employee and tell him he is terminated for the specific reason. As always, make sure you are following company policy and have checked any state laws before acting.

You will never get used to terminating an employee. We know management is logic, not emotions. But the fact of the matter is, if dismissing an employee is necessary, it must be done to preserve the store and its opportunities for

success. Simply knowing it must be done will never make
it easier.

2. TWO ASSOCIATES ARE OFTEN CAUGHT IN CONFLICT

Their conflict may be about sale competition, personality
disputes, simply not liking each other, or many other reasons. In any event, their discord will bring down the entire
store and its success.

This will follow a set pattern of events. First the fighting
associates will tolerate each other. Then they will begin
nit-picking at each other, then they'll tattle on each other
to the manager to gain a favorable position. Most times,
these two warring associates have very strong personalities, and they will do almost anything to gain the top position (the manager's favor). When this situation has escalated to a daily ritual, it's time to take action.

First, talk with each person to hear the complete sides.
Then bring them together; your conversation may sound
like this:

> Kim and Diane, it's clear that we have a conflict between
> the two of you. After hearing both sides, I have concluded
> that you are both right about each other. The bottom line
> here is the success of this store, so here is what's going
> to take place. You will both talk this out and work it out,
> put your egos on hold, and come to a solution to this
> situation. As I can't decide which one of you is better for
> the store, if you two can't work out this conflict, I will
> have no other choice but to dismiss you both. It's in your
> best interest and the store's best interest to work this out,
> so do it!

By forcing your associates to take responsibility for their
actions and grow up, they will.

3. HOW CAN I BE FAIR DURING HOLIDAY SCHEDULING?

Years ago, I was told something that has never failed to be true: take care of your associates first, and they will always take care of you.

We are not saying that you, the manager, should work every holiday situation, but give your associates first choice. A possible solution would be to list the holidays. Then, give your assistant managers or manager trainees first option on which holidays they would like to work. Continue on down in descending order through your full-time staff and finally the part-time staff. You, the manager, fill in with whatever is left.

In many retail stores, the holidays are the best times for sales and sales opportunities. You may find yourself fighting with associates for certain holidays. They want to work for the sales opportunities!

4. HOW DO YOU HANDLE INTERNAL THEFT?

Handle this problem as you would shoplifting: gather your evidence and prosecute to the fullest extent of the law! You really have no choice with this situation; you must take action. Your savior is documented proof of these problems—eye witnesses, photos, and so on.

Internal theft of time? How much time do you think employees steal each year from their companies? The daily flow of visitors and conversations with friends on the phone steal more than you may think. Several studies have concluded this time theft averages more than 6 hours for every 40 hours worked. This is expensive as six hours time $4 per hour equals $24 per week. At 50 weeks, this equals $1,200 per year. Multiply this by the number of employees on staff, and it's very expensive.

Many managers have found it necessary to have the employees deduct their play time from the schedule. This seems to cure abuse.

5. WHAT GOOD ARE RETAIL ASSOCIATIONS, MERCHANT ASSOCIATIONS, AND MALL MANAGEMENT TEAMS?

Good managers will become great managers if they rely on others to help them. These people are the support group of your success. It's their job to help you succeed, if you just let them. Often they are viewed as the enemy. But they are not! They will provide you with sales management ideas, promotions, events, merchandising help, and everything you ever wanted to know about your market and the customer. Use them every chance you get!

6. MY SUPERVISOR/OWNER WON'T LISTEN TO MY IDEAS. WHAT DO I DO?

In defense of supervisors and owners, you may not be saying anything. This statement is very hard to swallow! But when you call the home office, the district or regional manager, or owner, do you just complain about a concern? Or do you offer the what, how, and why and back up your idea with information and evidence to support your theory?

In defense of managers, is your supervisor so set in her ways and such a strong personality that you can never get through?

Continue to provide ideas to improve your chances of success. It is hard to communicate to someone who has a strong personality, but continue!

7. I DON'T BELIEVE IN CERTAIN POLICIES OF THE COMPANY, AND I HAVE A HARD TIME ENFORCING THEM. WHAT DO I DO?

It's a sure bet that you will never agree with everything your company does or wants you to do. But it's also a sure bet that the policy, rule, or regulation was set for some reason. Trying to know and understand the reasoning behind a certain policy can often allow you to see the light. Find out all you can before you pass judgment.

This situation is further enhanced when your competition has a reverse of the same policy. An example may be customer refunds. Your store has a no refund policy, while your competition has a liberal refund policy. As you may well find out, a policy was made just because. If you find out a certain policy hurts your business, work to get it changed. If you can't, at least you will know and understand why it is the way it is. Knowledge is a powerful tool.

8. WHY DOES MY COMPANY WANT MY STORE TO LOOK LIKE ALL OF THE OTHERS IN ITS LAYOUT AND WINDOW DESIGNS?

Actually, companies do this for two reasons. First, for store recognition. Our society is very mobile, and when people move to new locations, they will immediately recognize your store. But more important, they recognize personalities, products, services, customer appreciation, quality, store policies, and business theories.

Second, it makes your job just that much easier. Even though you may not agree with the look you must present, someone somewhere has saved you hours and hours of work. This allows you more time for sales, sales development, motivation, recruiting, and all of the other day-to-day activities that must be completed.

As you are faced with specific challenges, take the time to think through the options and see both sides of the situations. Above all, don't be afraid to ask someone for help. Often you are too close to the concern to see the answer, while someone else can see an opportunity before you do.

Self-Study and Sales Meeting Guide

"Knowledge creates confidence, confidence creates success, and success creates a desire for more knowledge. If this cycle is kept unbroken, your potential is realistically unlimited."

Gregory L. Will

T he following will outline a self-study and sales meeting guide. Don't put this book away on a shelf—use it!

SELF-STUDY

- Read or reread the entire book from cover to cover.
- Thirty minutes is then required each day, 15 each in the morning and evening. Be very precise with your time. Your time should be set when you are alone and you can concentrate.
- After you have read or reread the book from cover to cover, use a highlighter and mark the specific items, ideas, and examples that you now practice. Be honest with yourself.

- Start at the beginning.
- Each morning read for 15 minutes. Depending on your speed, this should cover 15 to 20 pages of material. Read silently to yourself. After reading, consider how you may use the information and try to incorporate its theory into your day.
- Each evening, reread the same material and, this time, read aloud. Then take a moment to reflect on how the day went and how the material was used.
- Repeat this morning and evening process of reading, considering, and reflecting until you have covered the entire book cover to cover.
- Repeat this process of morning and evening reading, consideration, and reflecting three more times.
- Review your progress. This time, using a different colored highlighter, mark the specific new items, ideas, and examples that you now practice. Again, be honest with yourself.
- Begin a new reading, considering, and reflecting period of morning and evening reading. This time, however, concentrate only on the ideas, items, and examples that you don't practice. As before, repeat this system four times.
- Review your progress. As before, use a different colored highlighter, mark the specific new items, ideas, and examples that you now practice.

Complete these periods of readings, reviews, and considerations until the entire book is highlighted.

You will notice the biggest changes in sales and management thinking after the first of the four reviews. After that, you will notice smaller changes.

- And last, but not least, don't put this book away on the shelf. Read and reread this book from cover to cover at least every six months.

SALES MEETING

Use this book to assist with your sales meetings.

- Your sales meetings should be no longer than 30 minutes. The following is a good guide to dividing the time:

  10 minutes of material presentation.

  10 minutes of discussion/role-playing.

  10 minutes of open discussion, any topic.

- Have your sales meetings weekly, bi-weekly, or monthly.

- Follow a sequence of events:

  Meeting 1—understanding the customer.

  Meeting 2—your first impression.

  Meeting 3—selling step 1, customer greetings.

  Meeting 4—selling step 2, qualify the customer.

  And so on.

- Enlist your staff to help conduct the sales meetings by placing them in charge.

Recommended Reading

I wish I had all of the answers, all of the time, everytime, but I don't. The following books on selling and management topics are recommended reading. Keep in mind, these books and their information may need to be customized to your retail environment.

SELLING

Hopkins, Tom. *How to Master the Art of Selling.* Scotsdale, AZ: Champion Press.

Mandino, Og. *The Greatest Salesman in the World.* New York: Frederick Felc Publishers, Inc.

Nierenberg and Calero. *How to Read a Person like a Book.* New York: Cornerstone Library, Inc.

Pegler, Martin M. *Store Windows That Sell.* Annual publication. New York: Retail Report.

Roth, Charles B, and Roy Alexander. *Secrets of Closing Sales.* Englewood Cliffs, NJ: Prentice Hall, Inc.

MANAGEMENT

Batten, J D. *Tough-Minded Management.* Des Moines, IA: J D Batten & Associates.

DeVries, Manfred F R. *Prisoners of Leadership.* New York: John Wiley & Sons.

Hanson, Peter G. *The Joy of Stress.* Kansas City, MO: Andrews, McNeel and Parker.

Kriegel, Robert J, and Louis Patler. *If It Ain't Broke . . . Break It.* New York: Warner Books.

Mackay, Harvey. *Swim with the Sharks without Being Eaten Alive.* New York: Ivy Books.

Index

Other excellent resources available from Irwin Professional Publishing . . .

CLOSE TO THE CUSTOMER

25 Management Tips from the Other Side of the Counter

James H. Donnelly, Jr.

(214 pages)
A sometimes shocking, often humorous look at encounters between customers and organizations gives you 25 ideas you can use to keep your customers coming back for more.
ISBN 1-55623-569-0

AFTERMARKETING

How to Keep Customers for Life through Relationship Marketing

Terry G. Vavra

(292 pages)
Gives you a clear mandate to help you gain category leadership in the radically changing marketplace of the 90s. Includes how to identify your customers and build a customer identification file.
ISBN 1-55623-605-0